Business Lessons for Tomorrow's Leaders

An Inspirational Memoir and Guide for Success in Business and in Life

Wendy R. Credle

Spanda Coaching Books
Copyright 2017

For Gianni
My heartbeat

Spanda Coaching Books
516 4th Street, Suite B
Palisades Park, NJ 07650

Copyright 2017 by Wendy R. Credle
Copyright fuels creativity, encourages diverse voices, promotes free speech, and crates a vibrant culture. Thank you for buying an authorized edition of this book and for complying with copyright laws by not reproducing, scanning, or distributing any part of it in any form without permission.

All rights reserved. This book may not be reproduced in whole or in part, stored in a retrieval system, or transmitted in any form by any means — electronic, mechanical, or other — without the written permission from the publisher, except by a reviewer, who may quote brief passages in a review.

The material in this book is intended for education. It is not meant to take the place of diagnosis and treatment by a qualified medical practitioner or therapist. No expressed or implied guarantee as to the effects of the use of the recommendations can be given nor liability taken.

Photo taken by Karen Riposo
Cover design by Ali Burke

Library of Congress Cataloging-In-Publication Data
Name: Credle, Wendy R.
Business Lessons for Tomorrow's Leaders (An Inspirational Memoir and Guide for Success in Business and in Life) / Wendy R. Credle
ISBN 978-0-692-81999-9
ISBN 978-0-692-82434-4

Printed in the United States of America

Sadbhagya
Great good fortune

It is my great good fortune that I am Gianni's mom.
It is my great good fortune that I am a daughter and a sister to Bob, McCall, Robin, Leslie, Julie, Erin, and Robert, Jr.
It is my great good fortune that I am a best friend to so many beautiful and accomplished women.
It is my great good fortune that I am a devotee of my beloved Guru, Gurumayi Chidvilasananda.
It is my great good fortune to have been able to offer this book to young people and professionals everywhere.

Acknowledgments
Karen Riposo – thank you for your beautiful photographs, spirit, and always showing up.

Sylvia Rhone, Chris Rock, Congresswoman Barbara Lee, Richelieu Dennis, Rich Kleiman, Skip Finley, Aaron Walton, and R. Donahue Peebles – thank you for your time, wisdom, and invaluable contributions.

Contents

Introduction

Chapter 1. Do What You Love, Find Your Passion   1

Chapter 2. Self-Awareness   41

Chapter 3. Communication and Relationship   66

Chapter 4. No Excuse for Bad Behavior   87

Chapter 5. Leadership and Accountability   122

Chapter 6. Time, Balance, and Success   149

Chapter 7. The Art of Giving   164

Introduction

"The great arises out of small things that are honored and cared for. Everybody's life really consists of small things. Greatness is a mental abstraction and a favorite fantasy of the ego. The paradox is that the foundation for greatness is honoring the small things of the present moment instead of pursuing the idea of greatness."
Eckhart Tolle

"What do you want to be when you grow up?" Remember that question? Even back then your ten-year old gut told you it was a set up. Then of course, depending upon your answer, your dreams were either praised and encouraged, or crushed, almost forever. And so, the programming began.

Some kids really do know the path they want to pursue. They grow up in families where everyone has the same or similar occupation, and so they come to believe that particular field is their destiny as well. You know children of cops become cops, doctors become doctors, lawyers become lawyers, and so on. Whether or not this is more a result of nurture rather than nature is ongoing debate, but that question is for another book, another story.

Some kids, like the famous comedian, actor, and writer, Chris Rock, without the influence of family, also know what they want to be at a very young age. Chris told me, **"I always knew since I was about seven or eight years old. I just loved comedians. When my family and I sat together to watch a variety show, everyone else would get excited when the singers came on, but I always got excited about the comedians"**. Or as Rich Kleiman, the Vice President of Roc Nation Sports and the Kevin Durant Foundation told me, **"my passion for sports happened as soon as I can remember being alive."**

I, unlike Chris Rock and Rich Kleiman, was not that kid. I had absolutely no idea what or who I wanted to be when I grew up. In my high school yearbook, *Boston Latin Liber Actorum 1983*, next to ambition I wrote, "To be happy and enjoy life to the fullest." It was the only thing I knew for certain at that time. I thought I was being deep. Well guess what, I was not and come to find out over thirty years later, most of the other kids in my elite high school felt exactly the same way. In the yearbook, the five Chans, one Cheng, three Chins, one Chomko, three Chows, one Choy, and three Chus, who all came before me alphabetically under the C's (we had a large Chinese population) pretty much all said the exact same thing in one way or another: "To always be happy", "To live, love, and laugh always", "To live a happy and successful future".

So I learned, thirty something years later, that we all want the same things. We all want to be happy and we want to be successful. But what does that mean? What does it mean to be happy? What does it mean to be successful? That is what this book is about. It's about discovering your destiny and getting to know yourself. It's about owning your power and excelling in business. It's about leading and making conscious choices. It's about maturity and carrying yourself with dignity and respect.

This book is designed for both beginners and old-timers. No matter how old you are, you can always start again. It is intentionally written in the most basic form so that every chapter and every lesson can be understood on any level. To help me guide you and tell my story, I have enlisted the help of a few of my famous friends who are at the top of their game as prominent business leaders, actors, and politicians. In their own, unedited voices you will have the privilege of experiencing the wisdom, advice, and philosophies of the following:

<u>Sylvia Rhone</u> — *President of Epic Records, CEO Vested in Culture*
<u>Chris Rock</u> — *Actor, Writer, Comedian*
<u>Rich Kleiman</u> — *Co-Founder and Vice President, Roc Nations Sports & the Kevin Durant Foundation*
<u>Congresswoman Barbara Lee</u> — *D-CA Congresswoman since 1998*
<u>Aaron Walton</u> — *Co-Founder Walton Isaacson Agency*
<u>R. Donahue Peebles</u> —*Chairman & CEO, Peebles Corporation*
<u>Richelieu Dennis</u> — *Founder & CEO Sundial Brands*
<u>Skip Finley</u> — *Broadcasting Media Expert and Pioneer*

I suggest keeping a journal while on this journey so that you can jot down your ideas and participate in the exercises. Keep a lighthearted attitude and don't take yourself too seriously. Have fun, and most importantly, believe!

CHAPTER 1

Do What You Love, Find Your Passion

"Follow your bliss. There's something inside you that knows when you're in the center, which knows when you're on the beam or off the beam. And if you get off the beam to earn money, you've lost your life. And if you stay in the center and don't get any money, you still have your bliss."
Joseph Campbell

Trust Your Dreams

Whether you have a passion for something but you are not sure what it is; or you feel like you have no passion for anything at all, it's all good. Life is not static and neither are you. It is full of moments when you feel happy and experience profound peace, and there will always be times when you don't. As you begin this book and your journey towards self-discovery and business mastery, I want you to pay closer attention to those happy, peaceful moments. Begin to notice what you are doing, what you are thinking, and whom you are with. This is your pathway. This is your guide. At some point, your thoughts will propel you into action and if the action feels good, you'll know that you're on the right path. If it doesn't feel good, then you know you're not. It really is that simple. Don't overcomplicate things and try not to worry.

We have all felt lost at some point in our lives and most of us have worked in jobs that we absolutely hate. As you mature emotionally and evolve spiritually, you will begin to trust yourself. Without the need to seek anyone else's opinion or approval, you will know when it's time to move on and test a different path. You will also know when it's time to do nothing, to be patient, and to wait.

Every stop along the way will be something you needed to bring you one step closer to your bliss.

Discovering your innate gifts is part of the process. Think about how boring your life would be if you knew everything about yourself, what you wanted, how you were going to get it, when you were going to get it, how much money you would make, or how much money you would lose from the moment you were born. Experiencing hardship is an essential part of your evolution. Hardship builds character and compassion. It makes you a more interesting person. The sooner you accept this as part of your journey, the less freaked out you will be when it happens.

I'm sure you have heard some of these questions before, but it's important for you to take the time to contemplate your answers. Self-inquiry liberates us from what we have created within. It undoes our subconscious conditioning and limited viewpoints. Ask yourself:

- What are some of the changes I wish to see in the world?
- What are some of my natural skills and talents?
- Is money enough or do I want more, and if so, why?

- How can I make my quest for success less self-centered?
- What about humanity, the planet, and other species; do I care?

In Sanskrit there is a word, <u>dharma</u> which has many meanings; among them are "right action", "duty", and "righteousness". Your dharma changes at different stages of your life. For example, when you have a child, you are in alignment with your dharma when you uphold your duties as a parent. You also have duties that you uphold as a spouse, sibling, or caretaker of elderly parents. If you enlist in the military, your dharma is that of a soldier.

The *Bhagavad Gita* is a seven hundred verse Hindu scripture written in Sanskrit that is known as the inspired song of the Lord Himself. It is the epic story in which Lord Krishna converses with Arjuna about his dharma as a soldier on the battlefield. The story opens with two armies facing off against each other. On the one side is Arjuna adorned in his chariot and ready for battle with none other than Shri Krishna himself as his charioteer. However, as Arjuna prepares for battle and looks over into the faces of his opponent's army, he sees his family members, relatives, elders, and teachers. His heart then melts with compassion and his manliness deserts him. Overcome with pity and full of sadness, he forgets about the honor of battle. Grief-stricken Arjuna asks Lord Krishna, "How can I kill them? How can I strike at my own heart?" Lord Krishna, astonished by Arjuna's dejected state of mind, explains to him the great truth. And so, the *Gita* begins.

There is also a Sanskrit word, <u>swadharama</u>, which is a little different from the universal dharma. Your swadharma is more personal to you, and that is what I am referring to here. This is your unique dharma. It is your unique law that springs from your nature and points to your specific purpose in life. Even Arjuna must never abandon his own sacred duty, his svadharamam. As my Guru, Gurumayi Chidvilasandana says, "Because each one follows his or her own dharma — which is different from any other dharma, which has its own variety, its own novelty, its own uniqueness — this entire universe is magnificent."

I've had the honor and privilege of knowing Congresswoman Barbara Lee since I was eight years old. Rep. Lee is a champion for peace and human rights. She was first elected in 1998 (D-CA) and has been, as described in her memoir, *Renegade for Peace*

& *Justice,* "a lightening-rod of political controversy". One of the things I am most proud of, and brag about all the time, is that Rep. Lee is the sole member of Congress to vote against the Bush Administration's authorization of military force in 2001 after the terrorist attacks on September 11th. If only her colleagues had listened. One has to wonder after over fifteen years of war.

At a very young age Rep. Lee knew that her passion was empowering people. Literally, from the moment she was born and forcefully pulled from her mother's womb, Rep. Lee knew that her destiny was to make life better for women and the poor. She experienced first-hand as a child and a young woman helping out the Black Panthers, the hopelessness of poverty and how it impacts the human spirit. She made it her life's purpose to do all that she could to help people find justice in a system that is fundamentally flawed.

While only in her mid-twenties, prior to her life in politics, Rep. Lee started her own facilities management and support business. She told me, *"I knew that I wanted to create jobs for people who were shut out of the job market. I wanted to enhance their quality of life. It takes a little creativity to start and run a business. I didn't have a business degree but I had a vision. I knew what I wanted to accomplish out of my business, and that was to create jobs. If you want to create jobs for other people, you have to start your own business."* Over the course of the next eleven years, Rep. Lee provided jobs for more than three hundred people.

    The first time I had to think about my career, under circumstances where I believed the decision had real consequences, was during registration for freshman classes at the University of Michigan. I remember my academic advisor telling me that other than one or two of the freshman required courses, I had to choose my other two classes based on what I wanted to pursue as a major in furtherance of my long-term career. Are you kidding, at eighteen! WTF! I thought to myself, "If I choose wrong I'll be stuck in a job that I hate and my whole life will be ruined. Ok, well here it goes." "So" I thought, "who makes a lot of money?" It popped into my head, "Doctors, I'll be a doctor, doctors make a lot of money." Did I really want to be a doctor? No, the thought had never even crossed my mind. Did I elect science courses in high school? Ah, no. Did I even like science? Ah, again, No. I took only what was required and I had no real interest in science. Did I like math? Yes, but I wasn't passionate about it.

So why did I tell this person, who obviously offered me no real guidance, despite the title "Advisor" that I wanted to be a doctor? Because I knew that money was important to me. I also knew that it was important to me to be independent, which at the time to me meant not relying on a man for support. Little did I know, again no "advising" whatsoever, that I was choosing one of the most rigorous and competitive curriculums for my undergraduate studies. And so, the hardship and the character building began.

My first year of college was one of the most challenging times of my life. I was homesick, lonely, and frustrated. I studied harder than I could ever remember and received a D on my first chemistry exam. I cried a lot and called my grandmother often. My saving grace was my college roommate, Leslie Boileau, who was also homesick and lonely. Instead of falling into despair, we blasted Phil Collins and screamed our heads off, "I can feel it calling in the air tonight."

After my first D in chemistry I knew what I had to do. I knew I needed extra help and I had absolutely no shame. I started going to my professor's office hours and tackling problems for extra help. I will never forget my chemistry professor. She was a stern, brilliant, little

Chinese woman who was no joke. She helped me tremendously and admired my tenacity. By the end of the semester, I started to get the hang of it. I realized that chemistry was like learning another language, and languages were something that I loved learning.

My second year of pre-med the focus was biology. Biology was not as difficult for me as chemistry since it was more memorization than problem solving. The turning point however of my short-lived medical career came during junior year physics class. I decided to bang physics out over the summer as an intensive course so that I wouldn't have to worry about it during the year when I had a heavier course load. Physics may as well have been advanced nuclear engineering or rocket science 101 — joke, you see why I dropped out. I knew immediately that there was no way I was going to conquer physics like I managed with chemistry. Our brains all work differently and it was absolutely clear to me that I missed out on the physics gene. Finally, I thought to myself, "Why are you doing this? You are not happy. None of this is coming to you naturally." I realized that not once had I ever dreamed of becoming a doctor. I had never played doctor games as a kid, can't stand blood, not even in scary movies, and couldn't fathom working in a hospital or around sick people all day. Definitely no higher purpose for me there, next!

    I packed up my bags and went home to Boston for the rest of the summer. Initially all of my friends were worried about me and thought I was having some kind of a break down; in fact, I was. I was having a break alright. A break out of hell and a break through to discovering what I was naturally good at and enjoyed. While I had no idea "what I wanted to be," I was definitely clear about what I did not want to be. When I returned to school my junior year, I switched my major to Communications. I loved the courses, the curriculum was more laid back, and my GPA was back on the rise.

    According to the revolutionary author Napoleon Hill, "the first principle of success is desire." We all want so many things, and that's good. In order to get what you want, you first must know what you want. Make a decision early in your life to be, as Hill calls it, the "master of your fate." Think about what you want, and act upon it. You are not committed to your choices for the rest of your life, but choose you must. If you don't choose, life will choose for you and you will be one of those people who describes their life using phrases such as "and somehow, I ended up", or "I got lucky", or "I'm unlucky", or "I'm never in the right place at the right time". You may want to take time to travel and explore the world. You may want to spend time at an ashram or monastery. You may want to spend time with a friend or at your parent's home to save money. These too are choices. You do have some say in the outcome of your life, but you must actively begin to explore. As commonly said and absolutely true, "showing up is half the battle."

Sylvia Rhone is the founder and CEO of Vested in Culture, and President of Epic Records. When she became the Chairman and CEO of Electra Entertainment Group in 1994, she served as the highest-ranking female executive in the music industry. Her historic appointment also established her as the only African-American woman in the music industry to ever attain such a title. Prior to joining Sony Music Entertainment, Sylvia served as the President of Universal Motown Records and Senior Vice President and General Manager of Atlantic Records. Needless to say, she is honored and respected in the entertainment industry as a pioneer and a legend.

My first job in the music industry in 1989 was as Sylvia's assistant. Since then our friendship has continued to grow and she is one of my closest friends. When I asked Sylvia about her career path as a young woman just entering the music business, she told me, "*I followed my dreams. I made discriminating choices about where I wanted to go. However, when I reflect back, I realize that sometimes they were not the best choices in terms of what my next steps were going to be. I could have been more discerning, but I was always passionate. If I had to give myself a piece of advice over the course of my career, it would have been to network more than I did. Networking would have been more of my focus.*"

The famous comedian, actor, and writer Chris Rock took it upon himself at a young age to create his own opportunity. "**I was always interested in comedy. When I was eighteen years old I saw an ad in the New York Times about a comedy club so I went to audition night. Like everyone else, I stood on line, picked a number out of a hat, and auditioned that night. They said I was good enough to go on late and be a regular. If they didn't hire me as a regular I probably wouldn't have gone back. They paid me about five dollars per night. That was a big break for me. Every break you get feels like a big break at the time, until you grow out of it and you realize I need a bigger break. I started getting small movie parts like *Beverly Hills Cop 2*, *I'm Gonna Get You Sucka*,** the *Joan Rivers Show,* and *the Arsenio Hall Show.* Those breaks came from people seeing me do Stand Up. It was the late 80s and there weren't a lot of young black comics so people began to know me. I was kind of ghetto famous."

To help you discover your passion, your purpose, your mission, or simply your profession, take some time to daydream. In my coaching work I make all of my clients think about and write down their dreams. As Joseph Campbell says, "Follow your bliss." When you follow your bliss, you naturally align with your purpose. What you consider bliss is distinct and unique to you.

Exercise

Sit quietly and imagine yourself professionally a year, two years, or five years from today, whichever feels most easeful for you at the moment. You are happy, there is no resistance, and you feel fulfilled. Money is of no concern. Close your eyes and feel this sensation. Allow it to permeate your entire body. Feel it in your soul. Want it with every fiber of your being. Now open your eyes and write out the scenario, in the present tense, at that moment in your life. Use only affirmative language and avoid absolutes such as "always" and "never". Use your five senses to be as descriptive as possible. Allow your poetic energies to carry you. What are you doing? Are other people involved? What are your relationships like? Where are you? Describe the joy and happiness you are experiencing and how it manifests in the outcome of your work.

The more you allow yourself to dream and consciously design your desires, the more clarity and insight you gain. You begin to know with certainty not only what you want but also, equally as important, absolutely what you do not. Abraham and Ester Hicks describe this as "scripting". You can have several different careers, hobbies, adventures, life-changing events in one lifetime. You don't have to succumb to the pressure or the idea that there is only one meaningful occupation that plays up to your strengths and passions. Script whatever comes to you as often as possible. You may see yourself as an executive one day and an award-winning screenwriter the next day. Napolean Hill tells us, "Every great leader from dawn of civilization down to the present was a dreamer."

R. Donahue Peebles is recognized as one of the most successful African American commercial real estate entrepreneurs in the country. He is the Chairman and Chief Executive Officer of the Peebles Corporation, which is a national, privately held commercial real estate investment and development company. Peebles Corp controls a multi-million-dollar portfolio of projects. Don was born in the early 60's during the Civil Rights Movement. However, in spite of the times, he still believed that his ceiling was very high and that he could achieve tremendous success. Unsurprisingly, which is certainly one of the reasons why he is so successful, Don believes that he still didn't reach high enough. When I asked him what piece of valuable business advice he would give his younger self, he told me, *"To see no limitations. I was responsible for tempering my ambitions and limiting my own horizons. My ambitions were not as big as my dreams, and I think there should be a correlation. While I was growing up I didn't see similar people of color achieve the level of success that I wanted or dreamed of achieving. I thought there was some kind of unknown, almost mythical limitation. For example, I never thought that I would see an African American President in my lifetime, or my generation. I thought, 'well maybe one of my kids could do that.' I made the decision that I could not be President and so once I made that decision, all my energy went into business. I didn't see the world evolving as rapidly as my dreams."*

Exercise

Go back to the dream that you wrote about in the previous exercise. Now re-write it and make it even bigger. Dare to be even greater. Eliminate whatever ceiling you may have subconsciously imposed upon yourself. As Don Peebles said, "I thought there was some kind of unknown, almost mythical limitation". Take a deep breath, expand your consciousness, embrace your power, and dream. Feel it, love it, smile at it, shout it out loud, do whatever it takes to make it real. Feel the reality of it and know that it is yours waiting for you to take charge and make it happen.

Arriving with Every Step

Whether you end up fulfilling your dreams or not, is not the point. As Supreme Court Justice Sonia Sotomayor wrote in her autobiography, *My Beloved World*, "Experience has taught me that you cannot value dreams according to the odds of their coming true. Their real value is in stirring within us the will to aspire." With a higher purpose in mind, you will know what steps you need to take in pursuit of your dreams. As you take on new endeavors opportunities will present themselves in ways that you could not have predicted. Take risks, experience temporary defeat, and expand.

   Rich Kleiman is the Vice President and Co-Founder, along with the legendary rap artist Sean Carter p/k/a "Jay-Z" of Roc Nations Sports. Rich told me that his passion for sports happened as soon as he could remember being alive. However, his journey took a lot of twists and turns. After dropping out of college, Rich had to figure it out. "I wanted to do this sports TV show about behind the scenes with athletes, so my friend and I went to Radical Media. Radical Media was able to sell the show with thirty-two episodes to ESPN. This was 1999 before all of the reality TV we have today, so it was groundbreaking at the time. We didn't really know what we were doing and someone asked, 'who is going to handle the music budget and license all the music?' My friend knew that I really needed a job and I really wanted to work on the sports side, but I agreed to do the music. They told me I had a $250,000 music budget. Looking back on it, knowing what I know now, it's impossible to license thirty-two episodes of music with a $250,000 budget. I asked them what happens if I don't spend the whole budget. They told me I could keep whatever I didn't spend. At that point, I had never even earned one thousand dollars, so my plan was to not spend a dollar. I started going to clubs and asking DJ's like Mark Ronson and Alchemist if they could also produce. I approached bands and told them to give me their music and in exchange I would get it on ESPN. I told them, 'I'm not going to pay you, but you will see your name on the screen and credits.' By the end of the year I got a nice check. I told everyone, 'ok I'm ready to get back into sports now' but they told me, 'no we need you to do the music for all our shows.' Next thing I know I'm in the music business.

    I ended up music supervising for Radical Media, which I never planned on doing. I was learning on the fly. We did TV shows, commercials, and movies. The artists I brought to the table were up and coming artists. It wasn't like I had an ear for new talent. Most of them came through my relationship with Mark Ronson. I started giving Mark a lot of work and he started blowing up in New York as a DJ. Then one day he asked me to manage him. All of a sudden, I'm a music manager. Mark is so talented that he started finding all of these young, unsigned artists and hanging out with Amy Winehouse. Mark and I signed two joint venture deals. One with Clive Davis and the other with Jimmy Iovine. Next thing I know I'm signing artists. Meanwhile, in the back of my mind

I'm still thinking to myself, whatever happened to my passion for sports.

While I was at Radical Media I met Jay-Z's manager at the time, John Meneilly, who wanted us to do something together. We decided to bring all of Jay-Z's footage from his show at Madison Square Garden to Radical Media. The next thing I know I'm producing Jay-Z's documentary, *Fade To Black*. All the while, I'm still saying to myself, 'how am I in the music business?' But then I started to love it. When I was growing up the biggest stars in New York City at that time were the music executives. Lyor Cohen, Puff Daddy, Jay-Z, Damon Dash, Andre Harrell, LA Reid, they were cooler than Michael Jordan. We all wanted to be one of them. When they were in the club, even the athletes wanted to hang out with those guys. So I thought to myself, 'you know what, I wanted to be in sports, but these guys are pretty cool too.' So now I'm officially in the music business. I'm doing business with Clive Davis and Jimmy Iovine, but in my heart, I knew that I still wasn't fulfilled. I met great people but I knew it wasn't my passion. Culturally sports and music are so connected so I was still around sports and everyone in the room knew that I was the sports guy.

It was like, Rich is in music, but he's the sports guy.

My relationship with Jay-Z continued to grow and I joined Roc Nation as a music manager. I was learning a lot and I was really good at it, but again, it wasn't fueling that thing. I liked doing deals, being in business, and managing talent. I thought it was cool and I loved the speed of it, but I didn't feel like I was the master of my craft. I didn't feel like I knew more than everyone in the room or that I could go head to head when it came to the art of music. At the end of the day, if you're in the music business, you have to love and know music. So when a few athletes asked me if I would help them with their careers because of my principles and the way in which they saw me manage artists. I jumped at the opportunity. Then I thought, 'this is what I want to do, let me talk to Jay.' Jay told me to hold off and wait because it was something he was already planning to do. Always in the past, whenever Jay to me to hold off and wait, it always lead to what he said he was going to do. He never told me something that didn't happen. So, when he told me, 'hold off I'm going to start Roc Nation Sports', of course I waited.

He started Roc Nation Sports and I started sitting in on the meetings. Honestly, I felt like I had been doing this my whole life. Everything I read in the newspapers. Everything I studied about the business of sports, contracts, and all of my knowledge of the players just came together naturally. I sat in the seat and I knew that I was a sports agent. I then told Jay that I wanted to do sports full time. He told me I could do it all, but I told him I didn't want to do it all. I told him, 'You can do it all, but I want to be the best at this. I want to be the best version of myself.' I wanted to get my life in a really good place and excel at something. I had to learn a new business. I had to build new relationships and network. I had to be a sponge again like when I was a kid in the music business. But this time it all made sense. I spoke the language and I fit right in. I knew that my calling had finally been answered. That was four years ago and I have never been happier. People around me now can't imagine that I was ever in the music business."

  No one ends up where he or she started, so just get started. Figure out what interests you and go for it. If you begin work in a field of genuine interest, you will excel a lot faster. When you like what you're doing, you naturally want to learn more. As your knowledge base increases you will become clearer and clearer about your next steps, your next endeavor, and your next passion. But you must start. You must start working somewhere, doing something now. Make a commitment and give whatever it is at the moment one hundred percent. Like Rich Kleiman did, meet as many people as possible, build your network, and build your most valuable assets: your skills and your reputation.

Everyone's journey is different. I needed to become a beach bum for almost a year before I figured out my first path. After finally switching my college major, when I graduated I still had absolutely no idea what I wanted to do. The only thing I knew with certainty was that I did not want to live in Boston, and that I did not have the personality or the maturity at the time, to take the administrative nine to five job my father had lined up for me at the telephone company. I didn't even know whether or not I wanted to stay in the United States, partially due to the fact that I had just returned from spring break in Barbados where I fell in love with island life and a Rastafarian guy name Zebi. The only thing I knew in my heart at that time for sure was that I wanted to know what it would be like to live on an island and I had to get back to Zebi. My plan was to spend the summer in Barbados while I figured out my next steps. I was young, in love, fearless, and other than my senior year college debt, had no responsibilities.

Fast forward seven months later and I was still in Barbados. I was making about fifty dollars a day teaching water skiing and working for a parasailing company. At the time that was a lot of money for a 22 year-old girl with very little responsibility. I broke up with Zebi after a couple of months on the island, and lived with my two dogs in a beautiful, simple, three-bedroom house across the street from the beach. I thought I had found paradise. I stopped thinking about my future and just enjoyed life. Then one night, while helping some friends bartend during happy hour at the local beach bar, I realized I was becoming lazy and that I was bored. It was then that the Universe conspired to deliver its message, as it always does when the time is right and you are open to receiving. That same night my first landlord from my first apartment I lived in with Zebi, approached the bar. "Wendy" he yelled, shocked to see me that night. I looked up, "Yes", I said equally as surprised and very happy to see him. He was always a nice man and I liked him immediately when I met him seven months ago. "I can't believe you are still here" he said, "Why are you still here?" I was stunned by the truth of his words and the look of disappointment on his face. He was right. What was I doing? Why was I still there? I was wasting away, becoming lazy, bored, and an island cliché. It was time for me to get it together and get on with my life. I had played around long enough. The next morning, I woke up feeling sad and heavy. The party was over. I took a walk on the beach and it came to me. I knew all along how much I loved hanging out with my father backstage at the concerts he once promoted. I knew as a little girl how much I loved going to concerts and how much I loved music. I knew my passion was to work in the music industry, and I knew that I needed to move to New York City in order to do that.

    I made a plan. The plan was to return to Boston for a year, work temporary job assignments to pay off the balance of my student loan, save some money, and then move to New York. I moved back to Boston and immediately landed a temp job. A couple of weeks later I started contacting a few of my friends who had moved to New York from Boston to let them know my plan. One of the people I called was my dear friend, Christopher Huggins, who was then a principal dancer with the Alvin Ailey Dance Company. Christopher was so excited about my plan however, he told me, "Wendy, you have to come now!" Huh??? It was December of 1988 and the Ailey Company was getting ready to go on their annual world tour. One of the dancers had an apartment in Park Slope, Brooklyn that she needed to sublet. I could have the apartment but I had to move to New York in two weeks. Without hesitating, I found myself agreeing and two weeks later packed up my little, black car and moved to New York City.

The next thing I knew I was alone in New York City, on my own with no job, no family, and no friends. I had only been to New York one time before and I knew nothing about the City. I used to dance in high school and college so I started taking dance classes at Broadway Dance Center to keep my spirits up and stay in shape. I quickly became friends with some of the other dancers. They told me about Backstage Magazine and how to book gigs. I started going on regular dance auditions and booked a job here and there to help pay my rent and expenses. I still had my senior year loan and an increasing mound of credit card debt so I continued to pursue my music dream. Even though it was the most difficult time in my life, I knew that I was in the right place.

After four months of pounding the pavement and meeting with various headhunters, I started to become really religious. If that's what you want to call it. It went something like this, "Please God help me find a job. If you do I promise I'll never do that crazy shit again." Literally on my knees in my apartment crying my eyes out, but somehow still determined. The next week while walking down the street, just returning from another disappointing head hunting appointment, I heard someone screech, "Wendy Credle". I looked up and it was a friend of mine who was a music major at Michigan. He said to me, "How are you? You must be looking for a job." I couldn't believe it. I felt like a desperate fool. Was it written all over my face? "Yes" I told him, "I want to work in the music industry." "Well" he said, "you have to go see Elaine Spurtell." (forgive me Elaine if I am spelling your name incorrectly). "She is a headhunter who specializes in the music industry." Are you kidding? I couldn't believe it. There was a person who actually specialized in helping people find jobs in the music business. I had spent months with several different headhunters and low and behold there was a specialist. For me it was a blessing and a sign. I turned down the forty thousand plus commission Cadillac job offer I was contemplating out of fear and desperation, and made my appointment to meet with Ms. Spurtell.

When I walked into Ms. Spurtell's office she signaled for me to sit down while she finished a phone conversation with her girlfriend about dieting and how it never works. Meanwhile, she had a huge plate of food in front of her. I was in the best shape of my life from dancing and suddenly felt the energy in the room shift as Ms. Spurtell glanced in my direction. "Oh no" I thought to myself, "It is not going down like this." As far as I was concerned, this woman held my fate in the palm of her hands and I was not going to blow it over a few pounds. I waited patiently for her to finish her call. Then without missing a beat, I jumped right in. "Of course", I told her, "I couldn't help but over hear your phone call, but if you have a moment I can give you a few simple tips that won't even feel like dieting but will make all the difference in the world." Fortunately for me, she could tell I was sincere and graciously accepted my offer. I gave her all my basic tips about portions, bread, alcohol, soda, exercise, etc. and then she said, "now little lady, what can I do to help you." The rest of my interview with Ms. Spurtell went so well that she made a call to her close friend in human resources at

Atlantic Records that same day, while I was still sitting in her office. I was so grateful I gave her the biggest hug and kiss. Having a college degree, enthusiasm, and pure intentions all paid off.

    A few days later I met with the head of HR at Atlantic Records, I wish I could remember her name. I walked into her office and there was a huge poster of Simply Red hanging on the wall. I told her the poster was a good sign for me. I explained to her that I had just moved to New York after living in Barbados for eight months and that I listened to that Simply Red *Men and Women* album, along with Stevie Nicks *Rock A Little*, almost every day while I was away. She told me Simply Red was her favorite band. We talked more about music and how it can change your life. We genuinely liked each other and she could tell that I was passionate about music. I aced my interview at Atlantic Records. I told her I was willing to work in any department, even the mailroom, just to get my foot in the door. She knew I meant what I said and recommended that I meet with Sylvia Rhone. She called up to Sylvia's office and scheduled the interview for the next day. At the time, I had no idea who Sylvia Rhone was or that she was on her way to becoming a legend in the industry.

Sylvia had just been promoted to the "Head of Black Music" for Atlantic Records and needed a new assistant. Those were the days when music was segregated by race and genre. I met with Sylvia, and that very same day she told me I had the job. She asked if I could start the next week. I thought to myself, "next week, how about now!" I didn't even ask my salary, it didn't matter. I was so happy to have a job in the music industry and I was determined to soak it all up and rise to the top.

It turns out that my starting salary was $16,900 per year. Do you need me to repeat that? Let's do the math. If you take out about $4,225 for taxes, that left me with $12,675 net per year. If you count fifty-two weeks in a year, that left me with $175.48 per week. Even for a single person I'm sure that was close to the New York City poverty line. It was barely enough money for me to live off of. I had to count my pennies every Friday so that I could catch the train to work. The train station attendant would get so pissed off at me for making everyone wait while he counted my pennies. Sorry but I had to get to work. I was there every Friday with a new sack of pennies apologizing to everyone in line behind me. Nevertheless, I was so happy. I was at that office first thing every morning with Sylvia and stayed as late as she needed me to stay. My job was the most important thing in my life and I loved it. I was learning, meeting people, and growing in a field that made my spirit soar. After four months, I received a pay raise to eighteen thousand dollars. When I got that raise it felt like a million bucks at the time. I think the train station attendant was just as happy as I was.

Be Prepared for Grace

Messages, messengers, and angels are everywhere. Universal good is the natural order for your life. You must believe and know that happiness and prosperity are your divine right. Be open, stay positive, and equally as important, be clear. All successful business people have a story about how it all began and the role that being prepared for opportunity and grace have played in their lives. Of course, there will be times on your journey when you experience fear and anxiety. But, a little bit of fear is good. It means that you care and that you are taking the process, and your life seriously. However, don't let it paralyze you. You must still take action, even if you take less action on certain days than others. Even resting is an action. Taking the time to care for yourself is part of the unfolding. You can't be creative and access your higher levels of consciousness if you're tired and full of anxiety. Look at your life and all that you have to be grateful for. Allow yourself to become more easeful.

My good friend, Skip Finley, has been a principal executive, board member, and consultant in the broadcast media industry for over fifty years. He was responsible for forty-seven radio stations, three nationally syndicated radio programs, and one satellite channel. As the Vice Chairman and member of the Board of Directors at Inner City Broadcast Holdings, Inc. Skip spearheaded the syndication of the Wendy Williams Experience and the Steve Harvey Morning Show. Skip's advises that you, *"Know everything about your business. I was lucky because I knew I wanted to be in broadcasting since I was eight years old. So that narrowed my focus and made it a lot easier. I was willing to do whatever I had to do to get into the business. In high school, I started stage crew because radio was a spin off from that. In my case there weren't a lot of people who did what I did. I was really good at buying and selling radio stations, and there were literally only nine other people in the country who did that. Sometimes there are things that you can't be taught. You have to get in and learn along the way".*

Aaron Walton is the co-founder of the tremendously successful, full-service advertising agency, Walton Isaacson. In 2014, Walton Isaacson was ranked one of the *Inc.* 5000 fastest growing private companies in the United States, and Walton was named an Agency Innovator by the Internationalist Magazine. Walton's boundless creativity and strategic acumem have made him one of the most admired executives throughout the Advertising, Brand Marketing, and Entertainment Industries. Aaron's career started as a marketing analyst for Pepsi right out of college. His story about landing his first corporate job illustrates how sometimes you have to create your own opportunities. When you have a passion, you don't let anything stand in your way. Aaron told me, *"Babson College was known for its entrepreneurship. In my junior year, I became the President of Student Government. One of my responsibilities was to go to all of the University trustee meetings to present the students' point of view on the academic calendar, and various other matters that affected the student body. At the same time, PepsiCo was coming on campus and recruiting. They were selecting students for an internship through a random lottery system. However,* they could only interview so many students on campus and unfortunately, I didn't make the cut. Normally, if they were looking for resumes I would have been selected because I was a good student. I was also involved in student government and a lot of other activities on campus. I really wanted to work for Pepsi so I waited for all the other students who won the selection in the lottery to finish their interview, and then I went up to the recruiter and gave him my resume. His name was John Henderson. I said, 'John I have to tell you that I really want to work for Pepsi and I know that you finished with everyone. Is there a way that I can drive to NY to meet with you?' He told me, 'come on in.' So, we sat there and talked in his office for over an hour. He missed his plane and I felt horrible, but he was so nice to stay there. However, since I wasn't part of the original lottery it would have been unethical for him to offer me a position. That didn't stop me and I didn't give up. I went back to a guy name Chuck Thompson, who was the head of the Alumni/College Resources, and I asked him, 'who do we know from Babson that works at Pepsi that I can write to and follow up?' He looked at me and said, 'You've already met Roger at the trustee meetings.' At the time I didn't remember Roger, because I used to meet *a lot of people at the meetings. The routine was for me to get up and present. People asked me a lot of questions, but I didn't get to spend a lot of time meeting people. Chuck said, 'let me write Roger a note' and he did. The next thing I know I received a call to go to New York for an interview and an opportunity to go through the interview process. Two days later, we had another trustee meeting and Roger was there. He came up to me and said, 'congratulations I understand you are going to be working for us; and that is how I found out that I got the job. At that moment, of course when I saw Roger in person, I remembered him. He was one of those really smart guy who always asked me challenging questions when I presented in the student government meetings, and always encouraging me to defend my position. I didn't back down and he dug that about me. That's how I ended up at Pepsi."*

Sometimes when you really want something you have to find your way. Aaron Waalton didn't give up, he worked his network and he created his opportunity. However, as the head of the student government, Aaron positioned himself to be in front of the right people, gain their respect, and build a reputation. When opportunity presents itself, you have to be prepared. You never know from whom or from where your chance is going to come. Always be professional and do your best work. Enroll in courses, training programs, whatever it takes. Make sure you are competitive. Whether it be technical, education, travel, or otherwise, make sure that you are skilled and qualified. Having an education, skills, experience, or an expertise put you in a position where you don't have to start at the bottom when beginning a new job. By starting one or two steps above the bottom you have a better chance of observing others in more senior positions and you have a better chance of being exposed to opportunity. It places you in the position where opportunity can see you. And then, don't stop. The executive who stops studying merely because she has finished her training is forever hopelessly doomed to mediocrity. The way to success is to maintain a continuous pursuit of knowledge.

Years later after a successful career at PepsiCo working with Michael Jackson, Aaron started his first advertising company which he later sold to Ominicon. A condition of the sale was that Aaron would stay on as a top-level executive at Omincon. During a corporate engagement with Earvin "Magic" Johnson, Jr., opportunity again presented itself, and Aaron seized the moment. *"I met Corey Isaccson at a* *meeting, not realizing at the time that he would become my future business partner. We both had this epiphany. We realized that the advertising industry needed to change the way it was doing business; both in terms of inclusion and in terms of its approach. So in response, we created a business plan called, <u>Creating the World's Most Interesting Agency.</u> We wrote an entire plan about how we were going to change the industry. A few months after finishing a rough draft of our business plan, while still working for Omnicon, I booked Magic Johnson to speak at an event in Dallas. I was on his private plane with him and a friend name Kawana Brown, who was running Magic's foundation at the time. Kawana was talking to me about how exciting the speaking engagement was and that Magic wanted to do more of them. I told her, 'well I'm not going to be at Omnicon anymore. I'm starting my own agency.' I had my business plan with me and I asked her to read it and rip it apart for me. I respected her and I wanted her opinion. I gave her a mark-up with notes in the margin and everything, a really rough, rough draft. She read it and she said, 'Oh my God, this is great!' Magic was sitting in the front seat of the plane. I wanted to be respectful of his privacy so I wasn't saying anything to him. I was just happy to be on his* private plane instead of flying commercial. So Magic turned around and asked, 'what are you guys talking about?' I thought to myself, 'well I have a once in a lifetime opportunity to talk to this amazing entrepreneur.' I told him about my plan. He said, 'oh that sounds interesting, can I read it?' I gave him my marked-up draft of the plan. Magic read the plan and he called me the next day. He said, 'hey I have been thinking about that plan, and if you want another partner I would love to be a partner.' That is how my new company, Walton Isaacon, started and we will be celebrating ten years in October.

Practically a miracle when you think about what was going on in the economy ten years ago. We were in a recession. Advertising and marketing budgets were getting slashed. All of my friends who I spoke to at the time about my plan for a new agency told me, 'Are you crazy, an advertising business, we are losing accounts!' It didn't matter. I was passionate and focused. I knew there was a missing link in the industry. Most agencies had been doing it the same way for so long that they didn't even know there was a different way to do it. You get comfortable, you get safe."

Definiteness of Purpose

Opportunity is everywhere, you just have to know where to look and how to recognize it when it is right in front of you. In spite of what you may have been taught to believe, you really can do anything with your life that you choose. It is a matter of choice, and setting a course of action to make your plan a reality. You are only as limited as your own mind.

I was at dinner recently with a friend who was celebrating her thirty-ninth birthday. She's a talented landscape designer who lives year-round in Martha's Vineyard. Since it was her birthday, I asked her what she wanted to manifest in her life over the course of the next year. She started by saying that she's feeling a little melancholy because she had fibroids removed a year ago and that based on what the doctor told her, there were four months remaining for her to have a baby before the fibroids started to grow back. She also mentioned that she wanted to be in a committed relationship before she had a child. After blowing off the idea of meeting some of the great guys that I told her I would love for her to meet, she then started to contemplate her career. She mentioned that she wanted her career to expand so that she could do more and be more creative. Once again, my wheels started spinning as they instinctively do. I told her that I had a friend in Miami who was one of the preeminent landscape architects in the world, and that I would love to introduce her to him. She Googled him and agreed that he was at the top of his game. I then asked, "Ok, how should I go about this? Do you have a website? How is it done in your business? Do I send him your resume?" She once again stalled and then said, "Well no I don't have a website because my work is so boring because my clients are so conservative. No, I don't have a resume. Well, actually I might want to switch fields altogether. Maybe do something with welding and installations."

From a distance, it's easy to see and understand why my friend was feeling melancholy on her birthday. She wasn't feeling as happy as she felt she should be at thirty-nine and believed her life was off track. How can the universe, in this case little old me or anyone else, help you if you don't even know what you want? If you don't have a definite purpose in mind, then no one else can have one for you. I'm so glad I asked more questions before I contacted my friend in Miami and wasted his time. If you're not prepared or certain about what you want to do, then you can't expect the Universe to figure it out for you. As you send mixed messages, so you will receive a mixed bag of tricks.

Dream big, be brave, and go for it, but equally as important be honest with yourself and be clear. Every day is a day either in furtherance of your dreams or away from them. While there are many factors that you won't be able to control along the way, there are still more that you can control. You cannot expect anyone else to do things for you. You must step up and do the work for yourself. Be determined about what you want and make it happen.

CHAPTER 2

Self-Awareness

"One of the most enduring of all the ancient laws of humanity is that we see the world not as it is, but as we are. By improving, refining, and defining who we are we see the world from the highest, most enlightened perspective. By mastering ourselves, we see the world and all its limitless opportunities and potential from the top of the mountain rather than from the bottom."
Robert Sharma

I offer this chapter to you for one reason only: So that you may consciously participate in your own delicious growth and expansion. In the Dhammapada, Buddha says, "Easily seen is the fault of others, but one's own is difficult to see." Self-Awareness is your greatest agent for change. We are all always growing and evolving. Perfection is not the goal however, we know parts of ourselves that could stand a little improvement. For example, I would like to swear less. Having lived in New York and worked in the music industry for over twenty-eight years, swearing has become a habit of mine. When I am excited and I start telling a story, I inevitably start slipping in a few choice words to heighten the drama, the humor, and the impact. It's fun and sometimes funny, but I know that it's not always appropriate or as feminine as I would like. Instead of beating myself up, I compassionately work on it.

Habits

Both success and failure are largely the result of a succession of habits. One of the reasons many people fail to become successful is because they lack the ability to focus and restrain themselves. In order to amass wealth and abundance you have to be able to focus. You have to learn to focus on what is most important, and to prioritize your actions so that they are in alignment with your dreams. If you scatter your energy by partying too much, talking too much, or even having too much sex, you have none left to be creative.

If you want to lead, your personal habits must demonstrate the quality standards you expect from your team, your customers, and your clients. You must strive to be the kind of person you want to attract in business and in your life. People have a tremendous amount of respect for discipline. I know that I do my best thinking, writing, and creating early in the morning. In college when I had to work on a difficult chemistry problem it was easier for me in the morning. When I write, the words flow more naturally in the morning. When I'm drafting a contract, I am more careful and meticulous in the morning. When designing a workshop, I'm more insightful in the morning. As a result, it has become my habit when confronted with a creative or intellectual challenge, to wait until the morning when I'm fresh and well rested.

Some habits are harmless, while others have the power over time to diminish the quality of your life. It's so easy to blame others, circumstances, your parents, or everything and everyone else for your unhappiness and lack of fulfillment. However, when you take a closer look at your daily habits, you will see a clearer picture of why and where you are stuck. For example, do you like to gossip? Do you procrastinate and put things off or do you get them done and out of the way? Do you drink more than three cups of coffee a day or binge on alcohol every weekend? Do you spend hours checking social media throughout the day? Do you scream and yell when you are angry? Do you lie or exaggerate?

To excel you have to turn the television and your computer off at night. You have to clean your house, your closets, and your office in order to elevate the energy around you so that you can think more clearly and attract more abundance. Throw out your old mattress and make your bed every day so that you can attract love. Stop talking about other people and focus on being a more positive person. Whatever it is, you know what you need to do. Robin Sharma wrote in his book, *Leadership Wisdom from the Monk Who Sold His Ferrari*, "Every time you avoid doing right, you fuel the habit of doing wrong." Look for ways to add love, gratitude, and kindness to your list of habits.

To become exceptional at what you do and earn more money, you also have to read and study your craft. For Rich Kleiman, beginning as early as the age of four, studying sports was more than a habit, it was an obsession. *"I was an athlete. You know everyone was an athlete in the making when I was growing up. But I was also a sports fan. A lot of times if you ask professional players who their favorite players were growing up, they will tell you that they didn't have time to watch. They were too busy playing themselves in the gym or at the park. I wasn't that guy. I never missed a game. I never missed Sports Center. I was reading Sports Almanac. There was no Internet back then so I watched every possible show there was and bought every book, magazine, and newspaper. When I was thirteen I started sneaking into bars to watch the games on Direct TV, because we didn't have it in our homes. I was literally an expert in sports, and it wasn't just in my own mind. Everyone who knew me knew that I was the sports guy, and that that was what I loved to do."*

Exercise

Take a moment and write at the top of a blank piece of paper three goals you would like to achieve within the next year. Then beneath each of your three goals make two lists, one labeled positive and the other labeled negative, of some of your daily and weekly habits. Those habits which support the fulfillment of your dream, go under the positive side. Those habits which keep you from fulfilling that dream, go under the negative side. List as many habits as possible and be honest. I mean at the end of the day, who are you kidding?

Attitude and Emotions

Emotions are infectious and they impact the workplace like a contagious disease. Effective leaders manage their emotions. They do not scream and yell when they are having a bad day. They recognize and respond appropriately to their own emotional needs, as well as those of their employees. If you want to lead you must learn to channel your negative emotions. I'm not suggesting that you deny your feelings, quite the contrary. What I am suggesting is that you honor your emotions and learn to express them in ways that produce positive results. You have to have a plan for dealing with your emotions. Consider the following questions:

- Are you overly critical?
- Are you combative or do take everything personally?
- Are you pessimistic in the sense that you have a tendency to expect and project negative outcomes, i.e., see the glass half empty?
- Do you have a tendency to take on too much responsibility, which then leaves you feeling angry and resentful?
- Are you a bully?
- Are you competitive or secretive?
- Are you passive-aggressive or manipulative?
- How do you respond when life feels unfair?

One of the ways to begin to manage your emotions is to asses those circumstances and people who trigger your negative responses. Pema Chodron is an ordained nun, author, and teacher in the Shambhala Buddhist lineage. She uses a Tibetan term called "shepna" which refers to the quality where we are hooked or caught. According to Chodron, "Triggering occurs at a pre-thought level. The mere rising of shepna is a natural experience for human beings and, in this sense, is in no way problematic in and of itself. What happens, however, is that along with the shepna, there is usually an urgency to do something in reaction, to get away, to say something, to somehow escape the discomfort of the feeling. It's not natural for us to simply rest in the hooked feeling, and fully experience what is there. Instead, we get carried away by its momentum."

In order for you to begin to redirect your knee jerk, emotional reactions into more positive responses, you must first identify them, and then embark upon the journey of identify what triggers them. This is a difficult lesson in self-awareness and for some of you it may be painful. If the circumstances are such that you cannot handle the discomfort on your own, I encourage you to seek outside help. In order for you to become the great leader that you were meant to be, you have to deal with your stuff. You can't run away from it because there truly is no place to hide. There's no shame in being human. You must get to know the things that trigger you. The amount of joy and peace you are able to experience will always be limited if you don't deal. In Douglas Abrams's book, *The Book of Joy,* while discussing emotional triggers with the

Dalai Lama and Archbishop Desmond Tutu, Archbishop Desmond Tutu spoke about emotional triggers. He compassionately told Abrams, "These are the things that you can train, you can change, but we ought not to be ashamed of ourselves. We are human, and sometimes is a good thing that we recognize that we have human emotions. Now the thing is to be able to say, when is it appropriate?"

Your negative thoughts about yourself and others manifest in ways that are counter to your dreams. As you get carried away in a chain reaction of negative mental story-telling, you act and react in ways that create detrimental outcomes. In the words of the beloved Mahatma Gandhi, "Your beliefs become your thoughts, your thoughts become your words, your words become your actions, your actions become your habits, your habits become your values, your values become your destiny." Part of becoming more self-aware is learning to pay attention to your thoughts and your feelings. You have the power to effect change and be a positive contribution to your family, your co-workers, and the world. I'm not saying that you will never have bad thoughts. I am saying that you have the power to notice them, and consciously decide to redirect them and see a situation or person from another point of view. You have the power to change your experiences, and as Gandhi says, "your destiny".

I know that one of my triggers is perceived injustice, to myself or someone else. My knee jerk reaction is to protect at all costs. As a lawyer, words come naturally to me, and trust me in the heat of the moment, I am capable of crafting a response that, in mind, certainly sets the record straight. Take that! This impulsive trait of mine is not good. I have had to offer many apologies as a result. However, because I know that I can be a hot-tempered Mama, I have learned to walk away from that blood-boiling moment and not respond right away. Of course, after I've had a chance to cool down, I'm usually in a better place to interpret the situation in a less personal manner and respond more appropriately.

Rich Kleiman told me that one of his personality traits that he is working on that he believes impacts his decision-making, is that sometimes he too takes things personally. Because he has a wife and two daughters at home, and like most of us has to sacrifice family for work, he takes his failures personally. ***"I'm working no matter where I am and I care so much about getting the job done, and getting it done right, that I take failures***

*personally. I do take people choosing not to go with
my agency, or not to work with me, or not giving me
that certain recognition that I deserve personally.
I wish I didn't because when I think about it and I
look at myself in the mirror I'm sure there are a lot
of people that I also probably don't recognize as
much as I should, or might not explain to someone
else why I didn't go with them as much as I could.
I'm about to turn forty in November. I would like
to care less. Not care less in the sense that I
won't be as passionate and still love my job, but I
don't want to feel personally let down as much.
Sometimes when you give in to that little bit of
emotion, you don't make the best decisions. It's so
easy to say don't mix business with pleasure, but
life, business, family, it all happens at the same
time, especially in the entertainment business. I
have to try to separate it at times, but at the same
time, I don't want to separate it too much because
you know that passion is why I think I'm so good at
what I do".*

Personality Problems

We all have parts of our personality that serve us well and are favorable for getting along and fulfilling our dreams, and we all have parts that do the exact opposite. Parts of our personality are innate. Other parts also have to do with the time and date of our birth, astrological sign, region, etc. Some parts are also a result of what we have been taught by our culture and religion. Then of course, we have our parents and those traits that are passed down through our lineage. This of course is not an exhaustive list of influences. Whatever the source, some of our personality traits we consider good and we like them, while others may be considered our problem children. The more you go to work on your problem children, the better off you and everyone else will be.

    I was coaching a Senior Vice President of a media company who had about thirty employees reporting to him. Over the course of our meetings, it became clear to me that the lack of morale he experienced from his department was the result of his staff's inability to communicate with each other. I offered him a free communication workshop with his entire department so that we could get to the root of the problem, and teach everyone at the same time strategic business tools for communicating more effectively. Instead of jumping at the opportunity, he continued on a negative spin, "It won't work. I won't be able to get everyone to commit. We all have different schedules. It won't change anything." He went on and on. As I tried patiently to address his concerns and organize the event, he continued to push back insisting that he was certain of the outcome. It was exhausting. Finally, I asked him, "Would you describe either of your parents as stubborn?" He lit up and responded, "oh yes, my dad is so stubborn." "Really", I said sarcastically. He looked at me confused. Then I asked him if he believed he was stubborn. "Oh no", he replied, "Not me." So, I gave him an assignment. I told him to go home and ask his wife if she believed that he could be stubborn at times. Of course, you know how this story ends. At our next meeting, he said that his wife couldn't believe that he was asking that question, and was astounded that he couldn't see it in himself. She said that he was one of the most stubborn people she knew and went on to easily give him a long list of examples. He laughed as he continued to tell me about the conversation. He was totally humble and realized that he had just experienced a tremendous opportunity for personal growth. He said he would begin to look for situations where he may have been getting in his own way due to his stubbornness. Now that it was at the forefront of his awareness, he could more lightheartedly see where his stubborn tendencies might be interfering with his success at work.

Chris Rock told me that one of his "flaws" when it comes to business is that he's not confrontational. *"I'm not very confrontational. Saying you're not egotistical sounds egotistical. But I definitely have a lot of friends who have to remind me of who I am in a given situation. I'm the oldest of seven, and when you're the oldest you're taught not to get your way. You always defer. You always make sure your brothers are taken care of. My friends have to remind me that 'I'm Chris Rock' and that I do have power. I can get what I want. I tend to not demand things until the last minute. I'm sure I could save everyone a lot of time if I just made the demands. My friends tell me, 'Do you know who you are? Do you know what will happen if you say x, y, z'? — and sure enough they are right. I'm the oldest child. That's the gig of the oldest; to keep the peace, to keep it moving. The youngest can be a baby and say, 'I want this' and get everything all the time. You can't be like that as the oldest."*

There are three less than desirable personality traits that tend to be most prevalent amongst us. They are being judgmental, controlling, and procrastinating. You may not possess any of these traits but even if you don't, it is almost guaranteed that you will work with or for someone else who does. The goal here is not to destroy your negative traits, but to have more compassion for them. The goal is to understand why you act out and how you display these traits, so that you can come to know yourself and what makes you tick on a deeper level. It's a process of becoming more accepting and more in touch with your own humanity. You will in turn also become more compassionate and accepting of others.

  Judgment is something we do to cause impurities to climb onto reality. Criticism is its closest companion, but judgment feels even worse. When we criticize someone, we are usually criticizing a behavior. When we feel judged, we feel like our very essence, our being, our soul is being held out for ridicule. It's ugly and it has nothing to do with reality. The last thing you want to do is open up to someone when you sense their judgment lurking around the corner. The worst part about judgment is that the person doing all the judging is limiting themselves as well, and probably in every area of their life. They are so worried about what other people will think, "less they be judged", that they're not living. Judgmental people are as hard on themselves as they are on everyone else. They impose unrealistic codes of behavior upon themselves, and then they go out and project those same codes on others. Judgment usually comes from a deep place. Often it is a result of having felt judged by your parents, religion, or culture. You are deluged with laws, rules, and expectations that are imposed by institutions, family, spouses, etc. Almost everyone has an opinion about how you should behave. As a result of so many established, outside influences, it's easy to lose touch with your own feelings and desires.

The second trait, which is one that I have to be most cognizant of myself, is controlling. Now the way that these problematic traits work is such that they are not always a detriment. Of course, I mention this here since having a tendency to want to be in control is one of my problem children. Depending upon the circumstances, your "negative traits" can sometimes benefit you and enhance your success. However, for purposes of this exercise, I want you to consider only the ways in which they cause problems or keep you from fulfilling your dreams.

We controllers are more comfortable when we are exerting effort and "making it happen". Sometimes we don't trust others to get it done or to get it done correctly. For me, the best way out of this trait is to do the exact opposite and to let go. When I find myself wanting to control the outcome of a situation, I take a step back and remind myself to surrender. Ironically, I'm better at truly surrendering in those circumstances where I feel most helpless. I do all that I can and then I allow the Universe to take over. When I start to feel jumpy, I breathe and remind myself to stop and do nothing. It has been my experience that the more I can truly be present to this state, the better things tend to work out; or if they don't, I feel emotionally triggered by the outcome.

Of course, as with all traits, there are different levels of moderation and severity. However, for the sake of clarity, let's take the extreme example. Also, because it's easier to learn from story-telling, this is a hypothetical story about a woman we will call Val. Val is in the prime of her life. She is married to a successful businessman, whom she loves. They have a ten-year old son. They own their own home and live an upper middle class, New York City life-style. Val is a Senior Director at her company and on track to becoming a Vice President within the next year. One of her strengths, according to her annual feedback report, is that she is the go to person in times of crisis. On the flip side, according to the same report, one of her weaknesses is that she can be too controlling as a leader. As part of her leadership development training, Val was given a self-awareness homework assignment. Her assignment was to ask her immediate boss, her assistant, her husband, and her son about her controlling personality trait. Her boss told her that there are often times when he wants to help Val with an assignment or a client, but that he doesn't because he feels Val would resent his help. Her assistant told her that he felt micromanaged. Her husband told her that he felt castrated and that it was easier to just let her do everything around the house because he felt as if things are not done her way, they are not done right, and she is never satisfied. Her son told her that he felt smothered. How do you think this feedback would make Val feel? How would it make you feel if you were Val or if you were her husband or son?

    The third and final trait is the one that will most certainly kill your chances for success, and that is procrastination. Procrastination is the opposite of action. All of your actions can help or hinder your energy. Not only do you have to put forth effort, you must act immediately. In his book

"Finishing On Top", Sherman Toppin diagnosed a condition lethal to finishing things that he coined "*Can't finishit*". Toppin describes some of the chronic symptoms of procrastination as "negative thinking, poor planning, wrong friends, bad-time management, insufficient funding, lack of interruption defenses, and overall weak resolve." Whatever excuses you may tell yourself, your procrastinating is minimizing your greatness. If mediocre is ok with you, then continue to put things off for another day or another time. On the other hand, if you care about your success and your life, and you want to feel proud of your accomplishments, then kill this trait. Any time you say to yourself, I can do it tomorrow or I will do it later, stop dead in your tracks and get it done. Face your fears, your doubts, and your insecurities. Step up to the plate. What you will find is that it is never as bad or difficult as you imagined.

Learning and Education

Learning is something that continues for the rest of your life. You've heard people say, "The older I get, the more I realize how much more I have to learn" - well, it's true. It's also humbling and that's usually a good thing. Even if you have a list of academic degrees, you should never feel as if you've completed your education. Great leaders and most successful people never stop learning. They have an innate thirst for knowledge and always want to be on the cutting edge of ideas, technology, and new developments in their business.

There's a growing sentiment that young professionals today expect too much too soon. It takes time to master the skills and emotional intelligence required to excel in business. If you are patient and diligent, you will receive the recognition and salary that you desire. With over two hundred fifty employees in four states and Japan, Aaron Walton has had a lot of experience hiring and mentoring talented young professionals. While discussing his younger employees Aaron told me, "*I think they want instant results. I think a lot of the younger folks I have met believe they should be the Vice President of Marketing within the first year or two of being employed. There are a lot of smart people, but I think the 'MTV instant generation' has not figured out that there is a lot of work that goes into becoming a Vice President. There are some brilliant, amazing people with great ideas. However, I do think that there is something to be said about the wisdom of working and understanding how the* dynamics of a work environment can change and shape an idea. How experience can keep you from making the same mistakes that you have made in the past. There are a lot of hard working younger folks who are willing to put in the time. But I have noticed that the expectation of sitting in your cube, to going to a C-Suite, is instantaneous. You are not ready for that yet. You don't know what you don't know, and you have a lot of time to figure it out. The more time you give yourself to figure it out, to make mistakes, and to learn from those mistakes, the better executive you will be. The more valuable you will be to potential clients."

Sylvia Rhone described her experience working with younger executives similarly. She told me, "It's mixed. There are some really disciplined, ambitious, smart people. And then there are some people working at the entry level who have a sense of entitlement. They want to move up the corporate ladder very quickly without learning the basic skill sets of business. Those people will definitely have a problem. But there are other people who are really dedicated. They are not above doing things at an entry- level position. There are a lot of young people who are dedicated and willing to make sacrifices, who just need an opportunity. They are unlike others who just want it to be gifted to them. Those who feel they are entitled are the ones I don't think will make it, no matter how smart they are."

Chris Rock and Rich Kleiman have a more envious opinion of today's younger generation. Chris, who like me is amongst the last of the Baby Boomers, told me he thinks, *"They're great. The fact that they even think about business is great. They are miles ahead of our generation, especially in show business. It's hard to believe how much business acumen these kids have. It's mind-boggling because I never thought like that at their age. I was raised to believe that if I could just get in the system, it would be the greatest thing in the world. These kids don't give a fuck about the system. They are like, 'we are the system. We make the system.' They join the system as a default. The kids of today that are in business are probably far more superior than any other generation. You're supposed to overshoot. I used to tell my agents, 'get me a job I don't deserve, don't get me a job I'm supposed to have. Why am I paying you?' Get me something where people are like, what the fuck, how did he get that!"*

Rich Kleiman, who is part of Generation X, told me, *"I think my generation lacked a work ethic at an earlier age more than this generation does. My* generation wasn't raised with the Internet and social media. We were raised admiring the new entrepreneur. We didn't envy the doctor or the lawyer. We envied the executive, the rap superstar, the basketball player, and the guy who started his own tech business and blew everything up. Those were the quick ways to get there. So, we wanted to get there quick by starting a fashion line or a magazine without realizing the work and time that was needed. We didn't know that no matter how much natural charisma, style, swag, people you know, or trust fund you have, that if you don't work hard, study your craft, and try to be the best at what you're best at, it's not going to work. Today's generation, the 'Millennials', have so many things they want to be. There is so much more that the digital world has opened up for them. Also, now that the digital world is incorporated in their curriculum at school, they are inspired to do so many entrepreneurial things. They study the tech icons and legends of Silicon Valley in school. School was not like that for me and my generation; it was the traditional stuff. I think it makes a big difference. If I'm in communications class reading a 1968 textbook of this boring guy, and then I see NY Magazine with Puff Daddy on the cover making millions, I'm conflicted.

I'd rather read that article. For our generation, you had to choose. I believed that if I wanted to be Puff Daddy or Jimmy Iovine then I couldn't stay in college. Those guys were carrying crates at twenty-one years old. I had to carry Mark Ronson's crates. To me that was how I was going to get there. I had to make a choice. I could go to Biggie Small's birthday party with Mark or I could go to class tomorrow morning. At the time, based on what I wanted to do, the party was more important."

Today the usefulness of a college education in light of the unforgiving student debt crises and the heavy burden it places on young people is ripe for debate, and both sides have equally justifiable arguments. It's a personal decision for everyone. My son is in his senior year of college and it has been a struggle for his father and me to pay his college tuition. It's important to me for him to graduate debt free. Since we are both professionals who enjoy a moderate middle-class lifestyle, I believe it's our duty to help our son with college. I know that there are some who struggle more than we do, and others who have no struggles at all. The inequity of it all is something that I think about all the time. Even though it's a hardship for us, I don't take for granted the fact that we are somehow managing to make it work. I value the benefits of an education beyond just having a diploma, and I know the step up on the ladder that I it provides. School teaches you how to think, reason, and make better decisions. Ultimately, life is about the sum parts of your decisions and each decision along the way takes you either closer to your dreams or further away.

CHAPTER 3

Communication and Relationship

"Silence is a great achievement."
Baba Muktananda Paramahamsa

Silence and Self-Control

Your thoughts and your words shape your beliefs, which in turn influence your success. Your thoughts create vibrations which you project into the energy around you. You speak the words which now strengthen that energy, and people respond accordingly. Your energy is powerful enough to manifest as your reality. For example, you know how there are some people who anticipate the worst possible outcome and in return, always seem to experience, what seems at the time, to be the worst possible outcome. When it comes to vacation time sometimes my sister Robin tends to be one of those people. She believes there is a conspiracy going on and that every time she goes on a beach vacation it will rain. Some of her constant refrains are: "I have the worst luck" or "knowing my luck it will rain the whole time", or more subtly, "I hope it doesn't rain". It's only recently that the Universe has decided not to conspire with her self-fulfilling prophecy and bless her with good weather on her vacations. Meanwhile, a more "positive" person with a more positive mindset could have the exact same outcome, even rainy vacation weather, but instead of experiencing it as the worst thing in the whole world, make it work in her favor.

In order to be successful, in addition to being mindful of your thoughts, you also have to practice self-control. You have to stop all of your sloppy talking. When you speak you let others know the state of your mind. One of the best ways I have learned to control the things that come out of my mouth is to keep it closed. The more you practice silence the better acquainted you become with self-restraint, self-discipline, and stillness.

Once a magnificent temple was built on an island. It held a thousand bells; huge bells; tiny bells. All fashioned by the finest craftsman in the world. When the wind blew or a storm raged, all the bells would ring and the music would send anyone who heard it into rapture. Gradually over the centuries, the island sank into the sea and the temple bells were submerged along with it. Soon all that was left of them was a legend. It was said that the bells were still ringing at the bottom of the ocean, and that they could be heard by anyone who knew how to listen. There was a young man who was so inspired by this legend. He traveled thousands of miles to the edge of the water. He was determined to hear the bells. He sat for days on the shore facing the vanished island and listened with all his might, but all he could hear was the sound of the sea. He made

every effort to block it out. But nothing worked.
The sound of the sea flooded his ears drowning out
everything else. He persevered for weeks and weeks.
Whenever he felt discouraged, he would visit the
local wise-men and listen as they retold the
marvelous legend. His heart would catch fire, but
when he returned to the shore things would be exactly
the same as they were before. Once again, he would
feel so discouraged. Finally, he was so dispirited,
he decided to abandon his quest. He thought,
"perhaps it is not in my destiny to hear these bells.
Perhaps the legend is not true." So, he made up his
mind completely to go home. On his last day, he went
to the shore to say goodbye to the sea, to the sky,
to the wind, and to the coconut trees. He gazed at
the vast blue ocean. Then he lay on the sand. For
the first time, he didn't try to block out the sound
of the sea. He listened to the waves crashing
against the shore. He let the sound of the waves
wash over him. He allowed his whole being to gently
slip into the depths of the ocean sound. A deep
silence seemed to emanate from the sound of the
ocean, infusing his consciousness, and he could no
longer tell from where that silence came, outside or
inside. Deeper and deeper he descended into the
depths of silence. Deep, so deep into its vault, and

then he heard it. The chime of a tiny bell. Followed by another, and another, and another, he could hear them all. A thousand temple bells ringing out in perfect harmony with the movements of the sea. He was in bliss. He was in bliss. Silence.

Exercise

Spend a whole day in silence. From the moment you wake up until the time that you go to bed. Choose a weekend, a vacation day, or any day when you don't have to interact with as many people. Carry a pen and paper with you for times when you must communicate a message, but try to limit your interactions as much as possible. The point of this exercise is to allow yourself the space to become still. The following day, preferably in the morning before you jump back into your routine, record your experience. Record your thoughts, your feelings, and the changes, if any, that you experienced within.

To be a successful leader, friend, lover, employee, or communicator, you have to master the art of listening. There is a famous quote by the Greek philosopher Epictetus, "We have two ears and one mouth for a reason, to listen twice as much as we speak." Listening while another speaks shows respect. One of the challenges of owning your own business is that you have to constantly focus on generating new business. It's every business owners dream to be able to sustain themselves on repeat business, but unfortunately that is not reality. Services end so you have to constantly hustle and be on the look-out for new business. When I'm pitching my coaching business to a prospective client, the one behavior that I can count on to help me nail the interview is listening.

One of the biggest mistakes sales people make is that they talk too much. It's so easy when you're focused on getting your point across to ramble on and try to get it all out. Especially when the stakes are high and you're nervous. When I'm being interviewed by a new client my mantra is, "listen and be patient". It's only by listening that I can discern the challenge the company is facing and where my services will best be utilized. You can't go into a pitch meeting with a preconceived notion about what that company needs from you. It's only by listening that you're able to understand exactly what the company needs and then when you speak, you can speak directly to those needs. Not all clients are the same, and if you want your business to succeed you have to come up with unique solutions for each client. The only way to come up with the perfect, unique solution for your client is to start off by listening so that you can pinpoint their needs.

Like me and most other entrepreneurs, Aaron Walton, is often pitching his advertising company to new clients. Aaron told me that when he goes into a new business pitch, the first thing he asks is, **"ok, what is the one thing that's keeping you up at night? Tell me what that is."** Aaron said that he has never solved a problem for any two clients in the same way. He told me a funny story about a scene in the first Brady Bunch movie that illustrates how important it is to respect your clients as individuals. **"Mike Brady, the father, was an architect and he was asked to design a building. He had all these different clients, but all the buildings he designed looked exactly the same. They all looked like his house. Even if it was a gas station or a museum, it still looked like his house. Yet, he couldn't understand why his business was failing."**

Conflict

"In true dialogue, both sides are willing to change."
Thich Nat Hahn

Conflict, in both business and in life, is inevitable. It's totally natural so there's no reason to fear it. In fact, the more your try to avoid a conflict, the worse it usually gets. Those folks who try to keep the peace all the time are usually repressing something. Over time resentment builds until they explode, usually over something silly, or at the most inopportune time. That is not peace. Repression is the opposite of peace. You have to find your voice and learn to speak your mind. However, there is a method to the madness. Along with a certain level of emotional maturity, there are also tools to help you navigate the dialogue.

In his book, *New Earth*, Eckhart Tolle wrote, "*What is an argument? Two or more people express their opinions and those opinions differ. Each person is so identified with the thoughts that make up their opinion, that those thoughts harden into mental positions, which are invested with a sense of self. In other words, identity and thought merge. Once this has happened, when I defend my opinions (thoughts), I feel and act as if I were defending my very self.*" When you're angry, obviously it's best to wait until you calm down before attempting to resolve a conflict. It's best if possible, to first work alone with your anger. Acknowledge that you're angry, and then try to breathe through it until you feel it subside enough for you to regain control and perspective. Loving speech and deep listening are the keys to restoring communication. When you act out in anger, you create more suffering and more anger for both yourself and the person to whom your anger is directed.

Chris Rock is essentially always working in a creative environment and since he's usually the boss, he has his own unique way of dealing with conflict. *"I'm usually the boss creatively on whatever I am doing. The people I work with usually have opinions here and there. I have my own little saying 'hear everything, listen to nothing.' I hear it out. But only listen to it if you feel it in your heart, and you think it is the exact right thing, but hear everything. People trip out. Anyone can give you a great idea, not just your boss. Even the janitor can give you a great idea. I'm willing to hear everything."*

There may be times when things are so bad between you and another person that you need the presence of a neutral third person to keep the conversation moving along in a productive manner. I'm a licensed divorce mediator. Divorce is probably the most stressful, and often toxic, area of discord that two people experience in their lifetime. As I'm sure you can imagine, the parties in a divorce action are often too emotional or too angry to resolve the issues on their own. Sometimes the same thing happens in business. The conflict can become so severe that it's best to have outside help. However, most successful business leaders learn how to resolve conflicts before they become that intense. As a leader, your employees, clients, staff, and customers will respect you more if you recognize and acknowledge conflict instead of pretending that it doesn't exist. It's your responsibility to draw out all the perspectives and encourage open communication and productive debate. Most people are inspired to find resolution under these circumstances. When you openly share your feelings, needs, and intentions, your staff will be more inclined to do the same and the relationship will be more authentic.

Rich Kleiman told me that one of his greatest leadership qualities is his ability to handle conflict. *"It's funny because where I can be emotional and sensitive at times, I'm the calmest dude in the room when it comes to conflict. There's no situation or emergency where I'm not able to stay level-headed, deal with it, get to a solution, and calm everyone down around me. In times of conflict and desperation, I rise to the challenge. I think it's important to let everyone get everything out.*

Sometimes it's ugly. People might have to yell and bark at each other, agree to disagree publicly, or storm out of the room. It's ok for me in my business to get all that out as long as the goal in the long run is to get to the right place. I definitely know how to reel it in once everyone has gotten their emotions out, and get us to where we need to be so that we can move on."

However, if you find yourself in an environment where there is so much negativity, then you should either look for a new job or, if you are in a leadership position, consider replacing some of your employees. Toxic environments not only impact results, but also the health and welfare of everyone involved. Of course, not everyone is going to like each other, that's just a fact of life. However, in a professional environment, everyone should respect each other and treat each other with dignity.

Obstacles to Communication

Three of the biggest obstacles to effective communication are: making assumptions, projecting your stuff onto other people, and the pitfalls of email. At one point or another, we all make assumptions. It's a natural tendency of ours as human beings. In the words of Neville Goddard, *"Whatever*

you may think of the question of free will, the truth is your experiences throughout your life are determined by your assumptions — whether conscious or unconscious. Assumption builds a bridge of incidents that lead inevitably to the fulfillment of itself."
What we think about something or someone doesn't necessarily make it true. The less we hold on to our fixed ideas, the better we will relate and connect to each other. The less presumptive we become, the more open and receptive we are to a newer and different experience.

    Projection diminishes communication because it imposes upon another person's reality. It's one of the biggest detriments to connection. You don't know what another person is thinking or feeling unless he tells you. We all have our own individual set of ideals, personal characteristics, and perspectives. Projection is especially harmful when the person projecting has negative tendencies. All of us don't walk around carrying a bunch of garbage. Some of us prefer to expect the good in people and in life. We don't project our stuff onto everyone and everything we see, and the last thing we want is to not be given the same benefit of the doubt. Projection eliminates the benefit of the doubt. It eliminates the benefit of anything beneficial for anyone or anything.

Email can be detrimental to communication because you can't read a person's tone through email. Whether you write "thank you" or "thank you!", since the person on the other end cannot hear the tone of your voice, depending upon their own state of mind they may interpret it the wrong way. For example, I once asked a high-level business colleague to contact another colleague on my behalf. At the end of the email I wrote "Thank you!!!" I put all the exclamation points because I was truly very grateful and I wanted her to know that. Instead, she wrote me back in way that made it clear to me that she interpreted my exclamation points in the complete opposite way. She interpreted my request as more of a command than my intended expression of immense gratitude. Fortunately, I know her well enough to read through her email and our misunderstanding. Instead of continuing down the email path of confusion and making the matter even worse, I picked up the phone and called her.

Most executives begin their day by either sending or responding to email. To set the tone of your email, pay special attention to how you begin. Don't underestimate the value of a simple "How are you?" or "I hope you had a great weekend." On the flip side, the impact and delivery of a negative or angry email also cannot be underestimated. There's nothing worse than receiving an angry email. Most people respond immediately with an angry email back. As I mentioned, I too am a work in progress and this was one of my problem areas. If unchecked, the negativity can go round and round until finally someone doesn't have the need to have the last word. When you lose your temper on email, you set yourself back ten-fold. I have learned the hard way that the amount of apologizing and backtracking it takes to undo an angry email is the biggest waste of valuable time.

Because we are now a society that often text each other more than other forms of communication, we each have developed our own sense of style, grammar, exclamations, umojis, and humor. Our friends may understand the underlying tone of our messages, but these same habits and idiosyncrasies do not translate well in the business world. When in doubt, be polite and be professional. Leave your humor and all of your little symbols out of your emails. Check your spelling, use proper grammar, and make sure that your message and intentions are clear. Most often emails are circulated, copied, forwarded, and otherwise passed around. Always keep this in mind when writing a professional email. If you need to communicate something confidential or otherwise sensitive, when in doubt, pick up the phone.

Gossip

Gossip is unmindful, usually ugly speech about another person. Whether it is true or not, when you utter or repeat negativity about another person it promotes dissention. When you speak, you always have a choice. You can choose words that create happiness, inspire confidence, and promote peace, or you can act small and gossip about petty things. There are usually multiple perceptions in every situation, and when you spread news that you don't know to be certain, you create a divide and discord amongst the group. In addition, when you listen to gossip, you support the person gossiping. Gossip is the poison that brings down the collective body and consciousness of your organization.

Challenging Conversations

Learning to navigate challenging conversations is one of the most important tools for you to master. It's so important that there are hundreds of books and workshops that deal with this topic alone. It's only by listening and exchanging different perspectives that you build truly authentic relationships with your colleagues. When we feel heard, we feel less combative and less reactive. Whether you choose to continue the relationship beyond the surface is fine, but at least the interaction will be respectful.

Unfortunately, being in partnership with others is not our natural instinct. It's always a conscious choice of human spirit that you have to practice and cultivate. Some people quite frankly are really difficult, however in the workplace, you have no other choice but to figure out how to get along and be productive. Your career and your success depend on it. The following is a guide for navigating challenging conversations. It's a combination of tools that I have learned and modified based on books that I have read, workshops I have attended or lead, my professional experience and training as a coach, my work as a licensed mediator, and my personal relationships. I have broken it down into six steps.

The first step to having a challenging conversation is to check your ego and assess its role in creating the conflict. Sit quietly and assess your feelings, the dynamic of your relationship with the other person with whom you are in conflict, and the desired outcome from the conversation. You may be angry, disappointed, envious, or hurt. You may be afraid to lose your job or a promotion. You may feel suspicious of the other person and their motives. You may feel indignant and self-righteous. Whatever it is, it's helpful to look deeply at your motivation, and what you perceive to be the situation from both points of view. This process enables you to see more objectively so that you can own your part of the conflict and be willing to acknowledge your imperfections. You must deal with your anger and tension before you embark upon the conversation. You have to work with yourself until you are able to approach the conversation from a calm, compassionate place. As Eckhart Tolle wrote, "Your ego when it wants something from another will play some kind of role to get its needs met. Whether material gain, a sense of power, superiority, specialness, or some kind of gratification - be it physical or psychological - the ego is the master manipulator. Whenever you feel superior or inferior to someone else, that's your ego."

    The second step is to schedule a face-to-face meeting with the person and inform him or her about the reason for the meeting. Schedule the meeting either in person or over the telephone. If possible avoid email for the same reasons we discussed earlier. By telling the person the reason for the meeting or appointment, you allow him the time to prepare. It gives him a chance to think about the conflict, and assess his role and his feelings. Also, it gives him time to get himself in the right frame of mind to have the conversation in a calm, constructive manner. In addition, it shows respect for his time. Often, we have no idea what is going on in another person's personal life so the timing may be off. It's common knowledge that "timing is everything" and proper timing can make a world of difference in the success or failure of your conversation.

The third step is to begin the conversation. Start the conversation by acknowledging the other person's point of view. Acknowledge the way you believe she may have perceived the situation and her feelings. If you feel you owe the other person an apology, begin immediately by apologizing for anything which you may be responsible; even if it's simply your contribution to the disagreement. There is nothing more powerful than an apology. Ownership stops the drama and earns the other person's trust and respect. However, make sure your apology is sincere. If it's not sincere, the other person will know and will have less trust or less respect for you. Speak with the language of compassion. Release your intention to punish. For example, you might say, "I have reacted or spoken in such a way that has created a problem between us, and I am sorry." It's amazing how often the only thing it takes to resolve a conflict and move forward is a sincere apology. In addition, it's helpful to continue to diffuse the other person's defensiveness by also finding a quality of behavior of hers that you appreciate and admire. Say that aloud as well. For example, "I have come to realize how difficult this project is, and I appreciate your skill and hard work." Then continue the conversation. Continue to tell the story from your point of view. Explain the conflict from your perspective and how you feel. Avoid blaming the other person or attacking her. Speak calmly and kindly.

The fourth step is to listen. Allow the other person to speak his truth without interrupting. One of the main reasons conflicts arise in the first place is because we don't listen to each other. This is your moment to acknowledge the other person, and be truly present to what he has to say and how he is feeling without preconceived notions. When you listen deeply you don't assume that you already know what the other person is going to say, and you remain open. You are listening with the purpose of helping the other person speak out and express himself. You are listening because you want to learn and clear up the conflict. Continue to listen even if the person demonstrates a lot of wrong perceptions, bitterness, or blame. Your job is to remain quiet, without interruption, and allow him to get it all out. Of all the six steps, this is the one that you may find to be the most difficult to master. It will be especially difficult in those instances when you disagree with everything the other person is saying, believe his perception is wholly inaccurate, or you feel attacked. However, it's the most important step in the process. In order to heal and forgive, we need to feel heard. This is how we soften and let our guard down.

    The fifth step is to ask each other questions and gain clarification. For true reconciliation, there must be a mutual exchange of dialog, information, feelings, and ideas. It's possible that you may not resolve all of the issues in one conversation. You may need to continue to have more discussions and practice listening and understanding each other. You may never agree on the same point of view, but you can at least come to an understanding of mutual respect. When you listen deeply to each other, you gain insight and you begin to see each other as human beings. With humanity, there is no space for anger or suspicion.

The final step is to come up with a mutual solution for the problem. Together come up with a resolution for how you are going to communicate and deal with the matter and each other going forward so that there is less probability that the conflict will continue to repeat itself. Agree that you are going to have more honor and respect for each other. Be patient with yourself, and be patient with the other person.

CHAPTER 4

No Excuse for Bad Behavior

"Your employees need your heart as much as your investors need your brain."
Jason Garner

Pride, in the Buddha's teachings, is one of the last five fetters that falls away when a person attains enlightenment. It's one of the twenty-seven mental impurities that the Buddha warned, can trip us up. No matter how old you are, it's never too late to learn how to behave. Courtesy and kindness go a long way especially, believe it or not in the world of business. Everyone deserves to be treated with respect, and the only way to earn respect is by showing it to others. This is your life and it's real. You're not making a movie, so stop all the drama. If you have a habit of acting like an asshole, then I promise you everyone knows you're an asshole, and whether you realize it or not, they probably don't like you. Having a degree does not necessarily make you wise, and it certainly doesn't make you superior to any one else. Being a role model is a privilege. It's a responsibility that should not be taken lightly.

Every day you are presented with opportunities to demonstrate your character. It evolves either positively or negatively, little by little over time. One thought and one action at a time. Don Peebles, a commercial real estate developer and self-made multimillionaire told me that he has a zero-tolerance policy when it comes to bad behavior. *"I hire people more so for their character than their skill set. I figure skill set is a learned behavior, character is developed over a life time; so I am a big believer in choosing people who have character. I don't yell, I don't diminish anyone who works for me, and I treat everyone with respect."*

Principles

We all have principles or values that guide our lives. One of mine is manners. It baffles me, how many people I meet on a regular basis who don't have basic manners. I mean the fundamentals. For example, in New York City where the fashion, entertainment, and banking industries thrive at the highest levels, I often encounter people who walk into a room or get on an elevator, and make no eye contact whatsoever, or acknowledge anyone else with a simple hello, smile, nod, or anything. For me, it actually feels unnatural to completely ignore another person. No matter how much potential you may have, it will be limited if you have no manners.

About ten years ago I was invited to sit on a panel of music executives at the Clive Davis Institute at NYU's Tisch School of the Arts. As part of the final exam, each student in the program was required to present a business idea to a panel of industry executives, artists, and lawyers for feedback and business advice. If a student was lucky, similar to the popular TV show "Shark Tank", I believe his or her idea could actually have led to an investment opportunity or job offer. On the day I was asked to judge, our panel of four was scheduled to hear three presentations.

The first two group presentations were a little underwhelming, but they went well. The students entered the room, said hello, introduced themselves, and then proceeded to present their ideas. They graciously accepted our feedback and thanked us for our time. Then came the third and final presenter. It was a young man who was presenting alone. He walked into the room and immediately launched right into his idea. He made very little eye contact and flippantly plowed through his presentation. Unlike the other presenters who made more of an effort, he wore jeans, a t-shirt, and sneakers. When he finished his presentation, he told us he was looking for an investment of one hundred and fifty thousand dollars, and that was the end. Out of the three groups, his idea was the most impressive, and I told him so. However, I also told him that he failed to greet us when he walked into the room, that his demeanor was somewhat cocky and privileged, and as a result, he did not display the kind of character that would inspire me to help him win. This may sound a little harsh to you, but I subscribe to the theory that if you really want to help someone, especially in business, then give your honest opinion. It doesn't help me if you just blow smoke up my ass, and in the long run, it won't help you. Whether or not my feedback ultimately made an impact upon this young man, I have no idea. However, if I did have one hundred and fifty thousand dollars to invest, he would have missed an opportunity.

At the end of the day, in business all you have is your reputation and it follows you everywhere. Even if you are the most skilled executive in your field, if you have a reputation for being difficult, arrogant, lazy, untrustworthy, unreliable, or just plain old mean, your success will be limited. The way you treat other people on a daily basis, even in those seemingly insignificant moments, make up your personality, your daily habits, and your long-term reputation. You have to be accountable not only for your results, but also for your behavior.

Sylvia Rhone told me that she is always acutely aware of her behavior, in and out of business, and the responsibility she has and owns as a role model. *"It's important for me, as the first black President and CEO, and the highest-ranking female in the music industry for a long time, to live like I have a responsibility. There are always mistakes you make and things you may do that are "off brand" so to speak, but if your bottom line, if your core feeling, is that you have a responsibility then you are accountable to that responsibility."*

Similarly, when you look at the most successful corporations in the world, they also have a culture and a set of core principles that guide their organization. Often it is found in the Mission statement. As you consider the different companies you may want to work for, take a moment to review their mission statement. Decide if their values are in alignment with yours. You will be happier and more motivated to find opportunities for long-term growth in an organization that you believe shares your core values. In addition, take some time to research the executive teams that lead the various organizations. Corporate culture starts at the top and unfortunately there are a lot of bad bosses out there.

When I asked Chris Rock how he dealt with people who behave badly in the film and TV industry he offered a unique perspective. *"My bosses change from project to project but just like everybody else,* whoever is paying you, is your boss. I can work with anyone that pays me honestly. But I would rather work with people who have kids. People who don't have kids don't have any place to go. They can work a little longer than everyone else. That compassion for 'hey I have to go', may seem like a little thing, but it's my child. If my daughter has a violin recital; in the world of business, it may seem like who gives a fuck about a violin recital, but it's my child so for me it's the biggest thing in life. I will work with someone who doesn't have kids, but I notice the difference. You're dealing with it on two levels: 1. Does your boss have compassion for the fact that you have to go to your kid's recital? and 2. Does your boss have to ever get the fuck out of there? In the ideal setting your boss is married and has a kid. Then you know they have to get out of there. But if your boss is single and childless, you're going to be there."

    I recently had a disappointing experience while representing a prominent businessman in a real estate transaction. He hired me as his exclusive broker to sell one of his personal residences. After two years of promoting and marketing his home as well as an excellent, all cash offer that he previously rejected, I was finally able to secure a second, even higher offer for him. The second buyer, similar to the previous buyer, also wanted to pay cash and close in thirty days. As is often customary, the offer was contingent upon an inspection. This was a dream offer and I knew the sale price would never get any better.

Because my client is a busy man, he has layers of staff people who handle different facets of his personal and professional business for him. In this particular case, his organizational hierarchy required that I consult with his Chief Financial Officer, Chief Operating Officer, Chief of Staff, two estate managers (the outgoing manager who had just been fired and the incoming manager, who knew nothing about the property at the time), and his real estate lawyer. This is a perfect example of what I affectionately call, "organized chaos" or as they say, "too many cooks in the kitchen". What started out as a simple transaction, ended up being a nightmare. After quite a bit of back and forth, the parties finally agreed upon a purchase price and the inspections were scheduled.

My client purchased the house over ten years ago and never really lived in it, so the inspection report listed $200,000 worth of legitimate repairs in and around the house. Thus began another round of conversations and negotiations that I had to have with my client's over-zealous team of executives. Unfortunately, since the price had been agreed upon, my client decided to remove himself from all direct communication and accept information only from his executive team. As a result, it became much more frustrating to resolve all of the outstanding, important details that we needed to negotiate before the lawyers could close the deal. This is one of the worst things a leader can do. Even though the owner was the only person who could make any of the final decisions, he put three layers of executive bureaucracy in the middle of the deal. It's like the telephone game. You start out with a message and by the time it is delivered to the decision maker, half of the information is jumbled or incorrect. In this particular case, it was even worse. Egos were involved, I didn't know whom I could trust, and I wasn't sure if my messages were even being communicated to the client/owner or if his executive team was taking it upon themselves to make decisions for him. What could have been a simple negotiation became a monsoon of mess. There are some business matters that are not meant to be delegated and something as personal as selling a house, is one of them.

Once the inspection report was done, the big issue on the table became which party was going to bear the responsibility for the $200,000 worth of repairs. The buyer wanted it in the form of a credit at the closing. Based on the facts that I have presented to you, if you are a fair- minded person, you would suggest that the parties split the difference and my client offer a compromise of a $100,000 credit at the closing. However, when your ego is as big as that of his Chief Financial Officer, something as simple and fair as that, does not cross your mind. Also, this was the first real estate transaction the CFO was navigating on my client's behalf, and I got the feeling he wanted to impress his boss. I suggested to the CFO and my client's passive aggressive, completely unhelpful, real estate lawyer that we split the difference and meet the buyer in the middle, but they refused. Instead, after nitpicking the inspection report, the CFO and the lawyer offered the buyer a fraction of what he requested as a credit towards the repairs, and suggested that the remaining percentage come from the commission that the buyer's broker and I were contractually entitled to receive when the sale was completed. Yes, that's right. I worked with this client for over two years. He's a multimillionaire at least fifty times over, and his CFO wanted me and my colleague to cover the deficit for the cost of the repairs on the multimillion dollar sale of his boss's home. Whether or not my client knew that his CFO wanted me to pay for his repairs, I cannot say, because unfortunately, as I stated before, he removed himself from the conversation. Let's just say that since he was somewhat of a personal friend who I'd known since he was twenty years old, it makes me feel better to give him the benefit of the doubt.

The buyer knew my client's net worth because it was published in Forbes Magazine. When the buyer heard that my client wanted his broker and me to cover the $175,000 difference, he was livid. Four days before the closing the buyer backed out of the deal, stating "he would never do business with a guy like that." Two months later that same buyer purchased another house around the corner for four million dollars more than the listing price of my client's house. Unfortunately for me I did not represent the seller of the other house so this was a huge financial blow. The buyer told his broker that he would rather spend an extra four million dollars than give my client two hundred thousand dollars, and that my client should be ashamed of himself for expecting me and the other broker to pay for the cost of his repairs.

Fortunately, it has been my experience that most successful leaders do not behave the way I have just described. That experience truly was disgusting and out of the ordinary. However, there are some people in positions of power, even if temporarily, who just don't get it. It can be frustrating and painful to watch people behave unconsciously. Losing this deal was a big deal to me. I needed that 6 figure commission to pay my son's college tuition. "But for" as they teach you in law school, the poor leadership skills of my client and the arrogance of his Chief Financial Officer, the house would have sold, and it would have been a great deal for everyone.

You will encounter all kinds of people at work and in all areas of your life. Instead of allowing them to darken your judgment with feelings of anger or fear, remember instead that everyone must find their own way to awakening and that the experiences they are having are an essential part of their process. Hold on to your light, and continue to be a positive contribution to the health of your organization.

Rich Kleiman has also had a lot of experience with people behaving badly during his journey to the top. *"I've come across bad people in business in the sense that I thought they weren't nice people. I have no problem dealing with those people when I don't think it's personal and I feel like they are not disrespecting or insulting me. You never really understand where someone is coming from. Where the anger is coming from. It could be their own insecurities, what they are going through at that point in their life, or that's just how they were spoken to as a child. I have a way of introducing humor and laughter into a situation and most of the time I feel like I can do that and not let it bother me. Then other times I realize it's ok to be sensitive and if it bothers me, to feel hurt. It doesn't mean that I'm not a man or that I'm not tough, because I know that I am. But that shit hurts when someone talks to you like shit and you look up to them. Or someone treats you like shit. It hurts you. It took me a while to realize that you don't know what someone else is going through, and you can't control them. Stay true to yourself and say how you feel. If you need to remove yourself from the situation, then you have to get out of it. If you're not happy at anything you are doing — a marriage, workplace, a hobby, then it's not worth it. For me it has to be fun. I find fun in the simplest things and that's the only way I can get through. Now when those people come around, I just walk away from them."*

Sylvia Rhone told me, "I return every call. Those are the kinds of things that to me are just respectful. There is no one too big or too small. Someone helped me out when I was getting started and at the end of the day, we all need each other because all of our lives and careers are entangled in some way. You never know where new business opportunities may come from. I think it's really important to give back and we don't do it enough. If you can lift one person up, then you lift up ten people. The 'dog eat dog' concept is dangerous and unproductive. There are some people who are not positive people whom I just distance myself from. One should never have a sense of entitlement because of what they do. There should always be a certain amount of respect for other people. Always work hard and not feel entitled. You have to appreciate your blessings."

Sylvia has always been one of my greatest business mentors and advocates. There are several small boutique management companies and law firms in the music industry, many of which are owned and run by women and African Americans. At one time or another we all have competed, along with the larger firms, for some of the same clients and some of the same deals. Sylvia is known and respected for being one of the few high-ranking executives who always looks out for the boutique firms, the "underdogs" so to speak, and particularly women to make sure that we have the same access and the same opportunities for success. When I told Sylvia about her reputation, she humbly responded, *"There are opportunities that you owe other people like you, so that they have the opportunity to be where you are. That's a responsibility that I take seriously and I try to abide by. As a result of my conscious efforts, I know the diverse complexion of the companies that I have Chaired and that I have given opportunities to people whom otherwise would not have had them because of their gender or color. I think that has opened doors for other skillful, talented people, and it will continue to do so."*

Executive Presence

You lead by example. In the same way that you did what your parents did and not what they said, your subordinates and peers will do the same. Like it or not, most people make judgments based on your physical appearance and how you carry yourself. You must be mindful of how you are perceived. In her book, *Getting the Best from People,* Martha Finney cited a study conducted by the University of Manchester and Monash University in Melbourne, where researchers found that obese candidates are more likely to be discriminated against in the workplace than their more slender counterparts. I know it's not fair, but you have to determine what you want to do about it. If you struggle with your weight, you have to decide what is most important to you, your career, your health, and possibly your self-esteem, or your self-righteous anger and frustration at the world for discriminating against people who are overweight. It's your choice, and the solution is within your control.

    The clothes you wear also make an impression. Not only do they impact the way others treat you, but subconsciously they also impact the way you feel about yourself. Buddhist monks wear robes not just for tradition but also to remind themselves who they are, what they are supposed to do, and how they should interact with others. There is an expression, "dress for success". You can determine for yourself exactly what that means while staying true to your own fashion sense and sensibility. However, "dressing for success" makes you more self-conscious in a positive way. It helps you choose your speech more wisely and conduct yourself in ways that set a good example to others.

In 2005 the National Basketball League became the first major professional sports league to implement a mandatory business-like dress code for all NBA players during the arrival and departure from games, and other times when conducting official NBA business. I remember the controversy the new law created and the outcry from the hip hop community and some of the more outspoken players at the time, like Allen Iverson. Iverson, who was notorious for wearing a do-rag and baggy jeans, told the Philadelphia Daily News "just because you put a guy in a tuxedo, it doesn't mean he's a good guy." It was a newsworthy debate that touched upon issues of racism and the unfair inference between hip-hop and being a thug.

"Allen Iverson was an anomaly", Rich Kleiman told me. *"I believe the reason why he was so annoyed with the dress code was because he honestly felt like he was being himself. He truly is someone who wore baggy jeans and sneakers, and to him that was dressing for success. That's who he was so it felt like a personal attack. When I saw his Hall of Fame speech I did think it was kind of inappropriate that*

he dressed like that, but you have to remember whom you are dealing with. That to him was what he needed to wear to celebrate the Hall of Fame. I think that dressing for success is important but, with an asterisk. I'm still learning that myself. You know I love to wear sweat pants and a t-shirt but I have also learned that dressing the part is kind of a nice icing on the cake to being the part. It definitely impacts how people look at you and how much attention they give to what you are saying. But more important than what you are wearing is how you wear it and the confidence that you exude. For example, there are days when Jay-Z comes into the office in a pair of jeans and a t-shirt. Now mind you the jeans and t-shirt are probably worth hundreds of dollars combined, but it's about the way in which he carries himself. The confidence in which he walks, he looks like he's wearing a suit; because he's so comfortable in his own skin. You don't want to look like a bum and you should dress well, but part of that is all about the way you choose to present yourself. It tells people whether or not you care about yourself and if you are comfortable in your own skin. I think that's important. If you're not comfortable in a suit, then that might not be the way you should dress. Dressing for success is having an outfit that looks good on, fits right, is clean, and makes you feel confident when you wear it.

Today we have the beauty of hindsight. Even though the rule still requires only business attire, most NBA players voluntarily wear suits and ties. Fashion has become an important part of their persona and the players carry themselves with a cool sophistication. Do the clothes make a difference? Yes, they do. They impact how you feel about yourself as well as how others perceive, and interact with you, no matter who you are or what profession you are in. Of course, I am not discounting any of the racial undertones or implications of the rule when it was enacted back in 2005. However, which employee would you rather hire? The one who shows up in baggy pants and a t-shirt, or the one who shows up in a suit and tie.

About ten years ago I was asked by a prominent producer who owned a small publishing company to meet with him and the President of his company about doing some outside legal work. The producer was a good friend of mine so I felt really good about the meeting. I remember leaving the house and not feeling comfortable about my outfit. My pants were a little too tight and too short. They would have looked fine if I had worn heels but unfortunately, I chose a pair of not so flattering flat shoes. My meeting with the owner went well. Then we walked down the hallway to meet his President. I remember standing in the President's doorway and feeling like I wasn't properly dressed and that I didn't look like a lawyer who could handle their publishing catalog. It's funny because I swear as soon as I had this thought I could see his President kind of scan my outfit. I'm a firm believer in energy and the power of the subconscious. I truly believe that if I hadn't had that moment of insecurity, the President would have never thought twice about my wardrobe. It was my energy that drew him into that space. The rest of the meeting did not go well. I couldn't focus and my game was off. They were professional and kind but I knew I didn't get the job, and I knew it was my own fault. I didn't look and feel confident, and it showed.

Meeting Etiquette

The way in which you speak and conduct yourself in group meetings are also opportunities to make an impression. Have you ever noticed that the same people speak in staff meetings all the time. Or, in other words, have you noticed that your so-called brainstorming sessions are all repeatedly "stormed" by the same brains. There are always a few in the crowd who think they know everything or are smarter than everyone else. The irony is that everyone else allows them to dominate the discussion even though they are all thinking the same thing… "I wish this guy would shut up" or "how can she be totally oblivious to the fact that she has said the same thing three times in three different ways and we are not stupid." How can you learn something if you never stop talking? It comes back to our discussion about self-awareness, or in this case, lack thereof. Make valuable contributions during meetings as they arise. Unless you are hosting the meeting, you do not have to speak in every meeting just to say something. When you honor and respect the purpose of the meeting as well as your colleagues, your voice will represent power, and your contributions will be better received.

Aaron Walton was the youngest executive at many high-level meetings when he worked at PepsiCo. He advises young executives to do their homework. **"The thing that I like that really helped me as a young executive was homework. I never went into a meeting unprepared. I would spend hours, sometimes days before a meeting going through the data and my position to make sure that I knew the answers to all** *of the questions. I would almost do mock debates and make sure that I had the data to back up my positions. I would put myself in my boss's position and I'd think, if I only have a little bit of time, what are the top three most important things that I would need to walk away with and understand so that I could make a decision. Then I would write those things down and make sure that I had the data to back them up. What I realize now is that because I did so much of my homework, I had a level of confidence that made my superiors feel comfortable letting me make a decision for them. A lot of it was about being prepared and knowing your stuff."*

A lot of people want to take short cuts. Successful leaders know the ins and outs of their business and they can always tell when one of their employees has not done their homework. You can tell when someone doesn't understand and hasn't really asked themselves all the questions. Do your homework and ask questions. Never be afraid to ask questions.

Bias

"May we all be free from distinctions of country, language, sect, and race. May we all have equality vision."
Wendy Credle

As human beings, we have a way of creating divisions amongst ourselves where there really are none. Our natural tendency is to measure everyone we meet by own our limited perceptions and experiences. We make judgments about everyone and everything all the time. The problem of course, is that we are flawed, and we are limited. What else do we have to measure another human being, but only by our own limited human mind and experiences. In order to break down these barriers we have to communicate with each other, leading with both honesty and compassion.

During the holiday season the Bergen County Board of Realtors of New Jersey has their annual cocktail party and dinner. One year I was invited by my friend Jade Stone to sit at her table with the rest of her friends and colleagues in the real estate business. One of the things I love about this party is the cocktail hour. It lasts about two hours so everyone gets a chance to really network. That's something to keep in mind. Try to arrive at business functions early during cocktail hour, even if you don't drink, so that you get a chance to network the entire room before you have to separate and go to your designated table. That way by the time you sit down for dinner you've had a chance to conduct your business and make valuable contacts.

Last year, all of Jade's invited guests, including myself, were African American. It just so happens, that our table was also the only all African American table at the gathering. As we started our entrée and were having a really great time, a mature white woman about sixty something years old approached our table smiling. She stood to my left next to where I was sitting. Quite pleasantly she addressed our table and asked, "Do you have any drugs?" Huh??? If this were a movie this would be the part where the whole room goes silent and everyone looks at this woman like she has three heads. "Excuse me?" I asked. I figured I must have heard her incorrectly. She repeated, "Do you have any drugs?" No one responded. We all looked at her like she was crazy. Then she said, "I have the worst headache and I'm looking for Tylenol, Advil, anything." "Oh" I said, "No, we don't have any drugs." Then she walked away. After she walked away we all looked at each other in shock. Me being me, I asked everyone, all of whom other than Jade I had just met that evening, "How many other tables do you think she stopped at and asked for 'Drugs'? Why do you think she chose our table?" One gentleman told me he was thinking the exact same thing. Another said he didn't even realize how offensive it was until I had just brought it to his attention. Another woman said that she was thinking that she may have gone to another table, but she doubted she asked for "drugs". The more we talked about the incident, the more I could see a couple of people getting visibly upset. So, here she comes again. As the same woman was about to walk past our table, I stopped her and gently called her over. Politely, I asked her, "Did you find your drugs, are you feeling better?" "No" she replied, "I didn't find any." "Did you ask anyone else at any other tables?" I inquired. I know I can't help it, sometimes the lawyer in me takes over. "No" she said, "No one at my table had any." "Well" I told her, "I'm sure you weren't aware of what you were doing but, as the only all African American table at the gala, we were offended by your selection of the word 'drugs' when you don't know any of us personally or professionally." "Oh" she kind of shrugged, "I didn't mean it like that." "No of course you didn't" I said. "You weren't aware that you were being offensive. That is precisely how subconscious bias works", I told her. "Now that you know" I continued, "I hope you will be more conscientious in the future." She looked directly into my eyes for the first time, and asked me my name. I told her, "I'm Wendy Credle, what's your name?" She told me her name, said it was a pleasure to meet me, and we hugged. When she walked away my new friends at my table looked at me in amazement. They told me how much they loved the way that I handled that. Emotions cooled and everyone at the event, even the "drug" lady, had a ball dancing the night away until the DJ had to kick us all out.

Unconscious or subconscious bias, whichever you prefer, is called "un/sub-conscious" for that very reason. It's not at the forefront of your awareness. We all have preconceived ideas and stereotypes. We have prejudices about other people based on the color of their skin, socioeconomic status, gender, sexual preference, religion, and everything else imaginable. Whether we have the best intentions or not, bias is there and it rears its ugly head before we even realize that we have acted upon it. We are not born biased, we learn it. We learn it from our own personal experiences and perceptions. We learn it from our parents, friends, associates, and the media. We learn it from our religions and cultures.

When I asked Rep. Barbara Lee how she handles the bias she has had to deal with for years as a

Congresswoman in Washington, she told me, *"I take it head on. It makes me very angry. It's probably the one thing that I have to consciously tell myself not to take personally. For example, there's an incident that happens to me a lot at airports. As a member of Congress, I cannot buy first class tickets but I can upgrade, and obviously I have a lot of miles. Since I have to travel back and forth from DC to California often, you can appreciate how over time traveling first class can really make a difference. However inevitably wherever I am at the airport, whether it be in DC or California when I show up in the priority lane, an employee periodically comes up to me and says 'oh no you have to go over there.' I respond to them 'please, this is my ticket and I'm going down this lane' and I just continue walking. In Congress it's a little different, because it's more subtle. Some of my white, liberal colleagues often need me to help them do certain things to further legislation. As a matter of fact, it just happened recently. I did everything that needed to be done to get a bill passed but when it passed, they didn't think my name should be included. I spoke to each one of them individually. I spoke to them specifically about racism and told them that this was a clear example of racism. They all apologized and agreed that inclusion was really important and that next time they would remember. It was clearly racial bias and not gender bias because half of them were also women. White liberals still do not understand racism. You asked me to do XYZ, I did it, and several times I had to ask you about my name appearing. Racism is alive. Race is a factor. In this country, the middle passage is here, right here."*

To effectively combat your biases, you first have to be willing to compassionately accept that you have them. We all have them. You have to be brave and consciously re-examine some of your stereotypically ignorant beliefs, where they have come from, and how they manifest in your life. This is another "hero's journey" in self-awareness. During those times when your impulse would be to respond stereotypically to a situation, or pass judgment, or even more detrimentally overlook a certain job candidate, take a moment to step back and turn within. Begin your journey and ask yourself, "am I being biased toward this person and what assumptions am I making? What can I do or say that would be different from my previous inclination?" You must consciously replace any biased tendencies with ones that more closely match your values. Even smart, well-intentioned people are influenced by bias because of the way our minds are wired. Your biases, similar to your habits, can be unlearned and changed but it takes effort and open, heartfelt, nonjudgmental discussion.

On the flip side, there are business opportunities that you can take advantage of when you understand human nature and our biased tendencies. I started working in the television industry within the past couple of years, and because many of the executives at the networks and production companies have limited knowledge and experience with other non-dominant cultures, there is so much opportunity for growth. For example, I'm executive producing a reality TV show about marriage featuring six, prominent, professional African Americans couples in the South. The concept was my creation and I handpicked the cast. I have an awesome production company partner that only has one African American woman producer employed full time at their company. Fortunately, my experience with them so far has been optimal. They value and respect my insight and the subtle authenticity that I insist upon as an African American woman. The relationship works because I also respect and value their expertise as one of the most successful production companies in reality television.

Statistics report that African Americans watch thirty-seven percent more television each day than any other demographic. All of those eyeballs add up to over a trillion dollars in consumer spending. African Americans should be an advertisers dream. Networks know this and the opportunities for black executives and producers in the television industry are growing. I'm not saying that only Latinos can write for Latin audiences, or that only women can write for women, however the stories are different and they tend to be told differently when told by an individual immersed in that culture and living that daily existence. We need that diversity of thought and perspective in the writing room as much as we do on the television screen.

Aaron Walton also uses his awareness of bias in the advertising industry to his advantage. He sees it as an opportunity to set himself apart from his competitors. **"In our industry and in our agency, I have always focused on making sure that the voices that were not traditionally heard, were heard. Making sure that black women and the Hispanic consumer segment were being recognized for their power. When I sat down with my partner to write our business plan, I was adamant that the only way that I would do this, was if part of the DNA of the agency** *was to make sure that we were looking at these different segments of the population; and that when we sat down with clients, we approached it holistically. So we had to have a deep understanding of Black, Hispanic, LBGT, and Asian consumer segments. I wanted to make sure that when I went to a client, they understood that the world was changing and it was time for them to face the world, in the same way that we wanted the world to face us. I wanted to make sure that the client understood that while you may not understand these segments, we are going to help you understand because they are going to be the future of your business. For example, I look at the work we have done with Lexus. I can point to some of their successes and say that we made it happen because we were able to show them the business case for why it is important, beyond the emotional or political correctness of it. Targeting African American consumers not only because they have a voice, and it's going to help the brand, but also because they matter."*

The conscious response to discrimination is patience. Of course, in the heat of the moment, this is typically the farthest response from our nature. Our emotions get involved and we feel personally attacked. Sylvia Rhone has learned the habit of pausing when confronted with bias. *"First you have to acknowledge that it's always there. No matter how successful you may be, there's always a feeling in the room, a "biasness". I have matured a lot so I am not as confrontational about it as I used to be. Some of those things are simply not worth my time, but the deeper things in the music industry are. It is not so much bias towards me, but bias towards the culture. For example, when I go to Europe for international meetings I have to deal with cultural bias in terms of the way they treat hip hop music. They don't understand it, but the only reason they do not understand it is because they don't hire enough black people in their companies. There's no one there to really champion the genre of music who is knowledgeable about black culture and how it works. As a result, there is a lot of money being left on the table. I have to help them figure it out. Instead of jumping at them or attacking them, I have to help them figure it out because it's not only important for them culturally, it's also important for business. On a personal level, I surround myself with people who understand who I am and why I am here. If you have a core group of people who understand you, it's easier to break through the clutter of haters. There are always going to be haters, so you have to be very strong and very confident about who you are and what you do. Right now the minority is the majority, whether it's LGBT, Black, Hispanic, Asian — those cultures are dominant right now. Because of technology, everyone is well aware of who the hot hip hop artist are. There is a huge appetite for the hip hop genre of music overseas, but nobody recognizes it or develops it to the next level. The Future record is an example of where the lack of diversity and appreciation for hip hop music posed a problem for our company. The record was number one on Spotify and number one on Apple Music. Apple Music was not global, but Spotify was, but because there was no radio play, the numbers were truly indicative of the influence of hip hop music, and the interest of the consumer. It's all just happening organically. It's a defining cultural influence that our international department needs to deal with. Pop music is their priority. They do not even think about putting marketing dollars behind hip hop music because there aren't people in the company who understand and live it. That is where I can be an influence, simply because I have the analytics to support it. I did it at Universal, and I am in the process of doing it at Sony. Now that I have gained their respect, I am able to change the culture of the*

company and improve the financials for international business at Epic Records."

Sylvia is in the fortunate position of being able to impact the diverse culture of her company. Music and the media are immediate connectors of people and cultures. There are no more influential mediums than music, film, and television on how we view each other and the world. Therefore, if you are a purveyor of these industries, you have a responsibility to make sure that your employees and your business represent the various races, genders, socio economic demographics and sexual orientations so that the representations are accurate and unbiased.

Nowadays, we have all learned to live with each other's differences a little more graciously, and that's a good thing. Younger generations are more understanding and appreciative of each other's differences. They are setting a positive example for older generations and other young people to follow. They need to teach their elders who have grown up in a more separatist environment. Separation breeds ignorance, which breeds discrimination. The younger generations are the generation that can change the world. They have the power to fill the world with peace and understanding. They have the power to stand up to ignorance and gently guide the world to a better place.

CHAPTER 5

Leadership and Accountability

"The task of a leader is to get his people from where they are to where they have never been."
Henry Kissinger

Some people are born leaders. They dance to their own beat. Even as a six-year old child when the teacher gave out chocolates, this brave soul would say, "but I don't like chocolate." The teacher would stupidly respond, "but everyone loves chocolate", and he would confidently reply, "not me." However, getting others to follow you, and inspiring them to achieve their own greatness is a completely different challenge. We are not born with these kinds of skills. Some of them come with time and wisdom, while others require tools and training. Over the course of many careers most of you will encounter bosses who are great, and unfortunately you will also almost certainly encounter others who are absolutely awful. Without perspective or some outside intervention, most awful bosses create awful employees who later become awful bosses. They pass down their less than stellar leadership traits to their subordinates, very similarly to the same way that parents pass down some of their less desirable attributes to their children.

Finding Leaders Worth Emulating

As the leader, your job is to attract the best talent, communicate the company's vision, foster teamwork, and set the standards for long-term success. It's up to you to provide the necessary inspiration for the organization to overcome obstacles, navigate through uncertainty, and accomplish the mission. Attitude is crucial for success in any endeavor and no one influences the culture of an organization more than its leader.

By the time they reach the top, most leaders have experienced some form of hardship and multiple forms of crises. It's been said time and again, "humility is one of a leader's greatest qualities." If you want to be a great leader you must embrace humility and go to war with your ego. Leadership is not about being clever or outsmarting your employees. It's about wisdom and compassion. Self-interest is shortsighted.

Sylvia Rhone was my first boss. I was her assistant at Atlantic Records for a year before leaving to become the East Coast Director of A&R at MCA Records. She was an inspiring boss and an incredible businesswoman. She was the first person to arrive at the office every morning. I often tried to get there early so that I could have the day laid out for her when she arrived. Whenever I managed to accomplish this nearly impossible feat, she would give me the biggest smile of appreciation. She answered and returned every phone call, no matter who it was. She was tough, but she was also kind, respectful, and fun. I will never forget calling in sick one day and the very next day when I returned to work, Sylvia asked me if I was feeling better. She made sure my responsibilities increased and she always let me know when I did a great job. I loved working for Sylvia.

A secure leader empowers her employees and encourages them to stretch and take risks. Sylvia described her leadership philosophy to me like this, *"I always think the head of the fish is like the body of the fish. I inspire my employees by my own work ethic and my own insatiable appetite to learn more about what I do, no matter how long I have been in the position or in the business. I inspire them to be creative and not feel confined by their job definition. I want them to learn as much as they can about all facets of the business. I try to empower my staff. Empowerment is important for a person to have confidence, gain knowledge, and expertise. I'm in a creative business, so I always encourage creativity. There's a quote I recited for a PSA commercial I did for VH-1 during Women's History Month, 'To Paint Outside the Lines'. It has broad implications and meaning, but I think it's important to paint outside the lines. I think that's the bed of creativity and leadership."*

Purpose

One of the differences between being a manager and being a leader is that leaders have a vision with a higher purpose, and they spend their days working towards that vision. Most employees are inspired when they believe their work serves a higher purpose. It's true that for an organization to be successful, it must have the right strategy, marketing, technology, product, financing, distribution, etc. All of the stuff they teach you in business school about running a business. However even if you have all of the right metrics, if you don't have healthy leadership, the organization will not thrive. According to a study conducted by the Hay Group, up to thirty five percent of the difference in business results can be explained by the day-to-day difference in the workplace culture created by managers.

Aaron Walton told me how his first boss, Rick Rock, inspired him as a young executive while he was at PepsiCo. *"I believe one of the best bosses I've had was Rick Rock. Rick was in charge of media at Pepsi. He transformed the way we looked at media.*

He transformed the way we looked at what we were doing and how it was connected to the entertainment industry. He was tied into pop culture. He was aware of who Gwen Stefani was before she was Gwen Stefani. He was willing to take risks. He was willing to push the envelope, and he was fearless in his approach to pushing the organization to do things differently. He also gave me a lot of room to do what I did."

Trust

It's the leader's job to instill a culture of trust and acceptance. When people trust each other, they don't spend time at work worrying about covering their ass or backstabbing each other. As the leader, you build trust by demonstrating your own vulnerability. You encourage honesty by taking chances, admitting when you are uncertain, and owning your mistakes. In his book, *Leading with Honor,* Lee Ellis wrote, "The painful struggles we would never choose often offer the greatest opportunity for personal growth, and personal growth is the only path to genuine leadership development." Turn your mistakes into opportunities by taking time to reflect on the setback, and then share the lesson with your team.

Sylvia Rhone and I discussed trust and accountability. *"I don't manage up, I manage down. I'm accessible to my staff no matter who it is, assistants, managers, Vice Presidents and Executive Vice Presidents alike. I foster an inclusive environment that allows people to learn more. I want to create a culture where people are happy and have no fear. I don't want my staff to perform out of fear. I also want the environment to be creative and intellectually challenging. I prefer more of a team, a family-like environment. I think that's the recipe for success."*

Richelieu Dennis is the Founder and CEO of the family-owned and operated, natural personal care product manufacturing company, Sundial Brands. Sundial is the maker of the number one multicultural hair brand, number two natural brand, number two bar soap, and top five bath and body brand in the country through its Shea Moisture and Nubian Heritage lines. His company, Sundial Brands, is a multi-million dollar company with a comprehensive portfolio of product offerings with America's largest retailers including Target, Walgreens, Walmart, CVS, Duane Reade, Whole Foods, Vitamin Shoppe, and several other independent health stores across the nation.

During our conversation about vulnerability, Richelieu shared a story with me about one of his greatest disappointments. He said that the experience lead him and his team to greater insight as to how to pinpoint their ideal customers and how best to serve them. *"Before we were successful, it took us years to find retail partners. Every time we went in to have a conversation the retailer would say, 'look the market is not ready. No one is going to pay for a natural product. You won't perform on the shelf.' They gave us all the reasons why not. As a result, I went back to my staff, pitched, and decided to lead the company in a new direction. I told my partners that we needed to create our own retail stores. If the retailers weren't going to give us the opportunity, then I believed we needed to create our own. That turned out to be a mistake. The mistake wasn't in trying to create our own retail stores. The mistake was in trying to own the real estate and run the businesses in the stores at the same time. It's difficult when you have so few resources to be able to do all three things: 1. own retail real estate; 2. retail a product; and 3. manufacture the product. Most brands and most companies only do one. The responsibilities are usually separate. Someone owns the retail. Someone does the manufacturing, and another company does the marketing and the brand building. I lead my company into all three things at once. I learned the hard way that it's best to focus only on the thing or things that we do best. I'm never going to be the best at real estate in New York. We lost millions. But to be honest with you, the money is not why I do this. That was not the most painful part. The most painful part was that I let the communities down where we were building. I let down the people who believed in us and supported our vision. That was the hard part. My mother and my sister advised me not to do it at the time, but I had a vision. I wanted to serve the community. The most liberating part of the experience was that we really learned how to serve our customer at retail. As a result of the experience, when we went in to partner with other retailers we were able to build a stronger case. Not just a case for why we should be on the shelf, but also how they themselves needed to evolve in the way that they served their consumers. We were able to help our retailers modify their messaging, their assortment, and their merchandise, so that they could be more successful. I would say maybe eighty to ninety percent of the success that we see today as a company stems from what we learned as a result of that failure.*

Leaders have to make tough decisions, however you can and should collaborate with your team. The more you encourage collaboration, the more trust you build as a leader and as a team. It's wise to encourage your team's input, creativity, data, and research in the decision-making process. Not everyone is going to get what he or she wants. However, having the best and the brightest provide their point of view will help you make the best decisions. Encouraging options and solutions also relieves the unnecessary burden of believing you have to figure it all out by yourself. The more your employees feel they are part of the decision-making process, the more committed they will be to ensuring its success.

Performance and Accountability

To stay viable as a leader you must perform. To get the results you want you have to build relationships and inspire the energy that drives accomplishment. As the head, you are modeling more than performance standards, you're also modeling your priorities and your integrity. You are the ultimate arbiter of accountability. If you don't keep your

promises and act in ways that are consistent with your highest values, your employees will view you as a hypocrite
and they won't respect you. Whether you're running your own company or someone else's company, you must be clear about who you wish to serve and why. You are responsible for the clarity of the organization's goals and how that message is communicated to your staff and your customers.

    Before I founded my executive coaching company, Spanda Coaching, I trained and worked with another small, family-owned coaching company for about two years. In the beginning, I loved the company and I learned a lot. There were a lot of really cool people who worked there, and I admired the work they were doing. I met the owner of the company, who we'll call Leslie for the sake of her privacy, while having dinner with mutual friends. She and I heard a lot about each other but had never met. We discussed her work over dinner and then she asked to coach me. I didn't really understand the work of a coach and I was curious, so I agreed. After about three months around our third coaching session, Leslie called me to suggest that I come work for her. She said she would train me and that she thought I was a great fit for her company. I was honored however, I told her that I didn't work for people but I would take a couple of days to think about it.

At that point, I had been running my own law firm for over fifteen years. It's not easy to go back to having a boss and having to be accountable for your time when you're not used to it. Yes of course, I would love a steady paycheck, benefits, and a 401K, however for me the trade-off isn't worth it. I know myself and I don't like being told what to do, how to do it, or when to do it. Not everyone can stomach the anxiety and the hustle of having to build and maintain a business, and trust me I have my days. However, the personal and creative freedom of owning and running my own business have become part of my DNA.

After a few days, I called Leslie and told her that I couldn't see myself working for anyone again however, I was open to creating a hybrid situation within her company that would benefit both of us. I went to her house during the Christmas holiday when business was slow to meet with her and her sister, who was also her partner and the co-founder of their company. I told them that I would work within their existing corporate and education departments by starting a new, multicultural division to help diversify their clientele as well as the students and faculty they were serving. Leslie's sister, who I'll call Becky for the sake of her privacy, was a little hesitant at first, but Leslie believed in me. We agreed that I would join the training program at the top of the year.

Over the course of the next year while finishing my training, I began to set up strategic pitch meetings within my immediate network in the music, television, and fashion industries. There were two heads of the corporate division of their coaching company. Becky was one of them and her brother in law was the other. I would set up the meetings and one of them would attend the meeting with me to deliver the pitch. The meetings with the brother-in-law went well and I learned a lot about pitching from both of them. However, Becky's personality was a little brash so depending upon whom we were pitching to, it didn't always work out so well.

Several months went by and I continued to set up meetings, but we weren't closing the deals. Then the day came when I was able to get a pitch meeting at BET Networks. This was a huge opportunity for my division and their company. I knew this one client could be worth hundreds of thousands of dollars in business. As the leading black entertainment television network, it was also a client that served a community that was near and dear to my heart. Becky decided that she would attend the pitch with me. I didn't want to blow this meeting so I asked her to go over her presentation plan with me. I could tell that she was a little off-put by my seeming to question her judgment, but I had a sense of what went wrong in our previous meetings and I didn't want to leave anything up to chance. I knew we would be pitching to six African American women and I knew there were some changes we needed to make for optimal results. I made a few suggestions about modifying the plan but as I suspected, Becky chose not to take them. She dismissed my concerns and told me to trust her. I in return told her that she should trust me, but she didn't.

The next morning we had our pitch meeting. Becky plowed ahead with her presentation. I could tell immediately that she wasn't connecting with the women in the room. At one point the head of HR even excused herself from the presentation to make a phone call. That's never a good sign. The whole thing was uncomfortable for me to watch. I was hoping Becky would pause for a moment to tune in to the energy in the room and make some adjustments, but that never happened. Instead she absentmindedly continued with her plan. She was a hard-edged, no nonsense, middle aged, white woman and she spoke with a strong Long Island accent. Her manner was pushy and aggressive. Although the women remained polite and went through the exercises, I knew we weren't going to get the job, and unfortunately, I was right. I left the meeting feeling disheartened and a little angry.

    The BET meeting was the beginning of the end for me in terms of my desire to continue my work with the company. The beauty of diversity is that you get an opportunity to learn about other people and other cultures. A great leader humbles herself and accepts that fact that the only way to grow and expand amongst other races and cultures is to follow, listen, and allow. Afterward the BET meeting there were a few other incidences at the company where I felt offended and dismissed as an African American woman. Since my job was intricately tied to the fact that I was the only African American in the company, it was important that my personal experience and perspective be respected just as much as my expertise. It became clear to me that I was not going to be heard or respected for what I had to offer and that the leaders of the company were not going to change, so a few months later we parted ways.

When I started Spanda Coaching, my intentions were clear. I wanted to render valuable coaching services to thousands of diverse, business executives who valued my holistic, practical, no-nonsense approach to success. I wanted to work with people and corporations all over the world from every background. I wanted to teach the value of humanity as much as results. When I circled back to most of the companies we had pitched to during my previous coaching partnership with the other company the feedback was as I suspected. Many of the HR executives I spoke to felt that they were insensitive and condescending and that the workshop leaders would turn off their employees. The work we were offering was extremely deep and personal so in order to get someone to open up and accept what you have to offer, they have to trust you. There has to be a connection. Most of the companies I met with while working at the other company, including BET Networks, ended up hiring my company and they are still some of my biggest clients and supporters today.

Know Your Brand

You have to know you brand. You have to know who you are as a company and whom you wish to serve. You have to have values and beliefs that you are not willing to compromise. If you don't have integrity as a leader and a corporation, your consumers, clients, and customers will know. Fakes don't make it.

With Spanda I had to start from scratch in order to market all fundamental aspects of my business. I had an established reputation in the music business so I never had to spend a lot of time marketing and promoting my law firm. However, executive coaching is a completely different business and how you market yourself and your services is far more important. I had to design my first website, create a brochure, write a new bio, and take new photographs. Even though I knew what I wanted and how to pull it all together myself, I decided to consult my friend Melanie, who worked in marketing and PR for a second opinion. The photographer who took the pictures, Karen Riposo, was a good friend of mine who I had worked with in the past. One of the reasons I liked shooting with Karen was because she was fun, and made me feel relaxed and comfortable in front of the camera. I invited Melanie to the photo shoot. Melanie suggested that I add a suit to the array of looks that we were going to capture for a more corporate look. During the shoot Karen and I could see and feel that the pictures we took while I was wearing the suit were stiff, and not representative of my true personality. I didn't like them at all. Melanie told me, "I need those shots in order to sell your services to more conservative clients like IBM or Microsoft." She was right, and I agree that those clients probably would prefer a more conservative looking representative, however I couldn't do it. The pictures felt forced and unnatural. I had to do it my way. Even though I needed the income, I told Melanie, that if the more conservative companies of the world didn't think I was "corporate enough" for them, then we probably weren't a cultural fit for each other.

For Chris Rock, his movie *Good Hair* was one of his personal favorites. Producing a documentary about black women and hair was special for him as a father raising two, beautiful, African American daughters. The movie did not do as well as Chris would have liked at the box office but he told me he didn't look at it as a failure. *"You want every movie to do better. I don't look at them as failures. I look at them as, that's where I was at during that time and I ask myself, 'did I get better?' It's only a failure if you don't learn from it. I would love for Good Hair to have been as big as a Michael Moore documentary. I did what I was supposed to do. Maybe I should have put it on television. That was up for debate, and we had the choice of either or. Maybe it would have been bigger as a HBO documentary. I didn't choose TV because I thought we had a legitimate shot at an Oscar nomination. We won Sundance and most of the films that win Sundance end up in Oscar contention. Unfortunately, that didn't happen. An Oscar would have been nice. It's not per se about the award as it is about the nomination and the fact that it makes the next thing that much easier."*

In their book, *Attracting Perfect Customers*, Stacey Hall and Jan Brogniez, wrote a story about a lighthouse that they call, the Lighthouse Test. The message of this story is so critical to running a business that I wanted to include it in its original, unedited form. This is their story: "Imagine a lighthouse standing strong and tall on the rocky shore of a beautiful harbor. The water is calm, the sky is blue, and many boats are out at sea. But off in the distance a storm cloud is forming. It approaches the shore very quickly. The sky is getter darker, the waves are getting rougher, and many of the boats are being tossed about on the water. As the rain and wind puck up strength, the power of the beam of light emanating from the lighthouse increases. The darker the skies become, the brighter the light shines to provide safety and security in the midst of the storm. Notice that not all of the boats need this beam of light to guide them to safety. Some have confident captains and crews, and some are fully equipped to manage through the storms safely and effectively. Now imagine that the lighthouse gets upset because some of the boats are choosing to follow their own path. The lighthouse feels that it is not successful if its light is not guiding all of the boats in the sea. It sprouts arms and legs and runs up and down the beach acting light a searchlight, doing its best to catch the attention of all the boat captains, attempting to encourage more of them to depend on its light." The result, as explained by Hall and Brogniez, is that "very few boats would be served well or at all by the lighthouse. It takes a lot of energy to look for people to serve. The Lighthouse - your most perfect customers - are patiently waiting for you. In fact, they are looking for you and are counting on you to stand still so that they can find you at the most perfect time and place."

Aaron Walton, who is a brand and marketing expert, described his philosophy, *"When we first started the agency, there were clients that we took on largely because of our need to generate revenue to cover our expenses. What you don't realize during times like these, is that sometimes you are better off by saying no to a piece of business if it's not the right cultural fit. Yes, even if it will generate revenue for your company. Ultimately, it's not worth the opportunity cost in terms of staff morale and alignment with your company's philosophy. The 'perfect customers' for me are Lexus and Toyota because they do an outstanding job of making sure their support agencies, like ours, feel like true partners instead of vendors. That distinction is critical. It helps define our relationship in such a way that we both feel we have a joint responsibility to build each other's business and focus on shared long-term goals. We each feel a responsibility to ensure that both of our companies thrive and prosper. This is a very smart strategy because like any true successful partnership, both parties should rise with the tide."*

Mentoring and Sponsorship

Great leaders beget great leaders. They are as concerned about the careers of their employees as they are about the business. I have several friends and colleagues in the music industry who have thrived in their careers under the leadership and guidance of Andre Harrell, Russell Simmons, Lyor Cohen, Sylvia Rhone, Julie Greenwald, and Craig Kallman. Fortunately for me I have also had the good fortune to know all of them personally and gain invaluable knowledge and insight. I also know that all of them habitually focused on their collective teams being number one, rather than just their own individual results. They gave credit and acknowledged the contributions of their staff.

    Sponsors are something you create for yourself. If you don't have anyone directly within your company looking out for you, guiding you, and teaching you, then you have to take it upon yourself to gain that knowledge and create your network wherever and whenever you can. Rich Kleiman is a perfect example of an executive who took advantage of all of his opportunities. He told me, **"I want so much and this book is going to be so helpful for people because I didn't have anything like this, but I was able to be around so many of the people that you are interviewing and learn from them. Every time I sat with Lyor Cohen, I asked him questions and I listened. We may have been at the Spotted Pig but I still paid close attention. I loved the perks of** *being friends and socializing with Jay-Z and going out, but when he told stories I listened."*

People know when you care about them and loyalty goes both ways. You don't have to be the smartest person in the room, or know everything there is to know in your business. However, it's crucial to know how to recognize and nurture the talents of others. There's no greater reward as a leader than to watch the young professional women and men that you have guided and mentored, go on to become successful leaders and entrepreneurs.

Sylvia Rhone told me, *"I'm really proud of the executives that I brought in and the opportunities that I was able to give them. For example, at Atlantic Records I hired Merlin Bob as the head of A&R and Gina Harrell as the head of Production. In all of the companies I have lead, we have always had talented people in high-level executive positions. I believe that many of them would not have been given those opportunities if I hadn't been in the position to open the door for them. I love putting executive teams together because at the end of the day, it's all about that team. It's never about you. As soon as you lose sight and think it's all about you, the company will fall apart. You have to invest a lot of time in building and supporting your staff. Make sure that you bring people up all the time, and that they have mobility within the company to feel inspired and grow. I love to see executives grow just as much as the success of the artists we work with."*

Decision Making

In today's workplace where change is occurring at an increasingly rapid rate, as the leader you must have a strategy to address the negative emotions these changes evoke. In his book, *Leading With Honor*, Lee Ellis wrote, "Anyone can steer the ship through calm waters. The real captains take it through the storms." In the music industry alone, the consolidation has been catastrophic. Record companies used to make a lot of money on record sales and that has change drastically. Because of the Internet downloading and streaming, most artists no longer see a record royalty. As a result, there are fewer record companies, fewer record deals, and smaller staffs.

In so many industries the landscape as we used to know it has changed and continues to change every single day. There's very little room for error. As a result, your employees must rise to the occasion. Excellence is a must and often you will have to make tough decisions. As the leader, you can't afford to keep employees who are not qualified, or who have values that are not in alignment with the culture of your organization. It's not easy to fire someone. To knowingly take away their means of supporting themselves is a big decision. However sometimes it's necessary and often for the best or else it can be destructive to the rest of your organization. Jack Welsh, the Chairman of General Electric said, "one of the hardest things to do is to fire somebody'. It's difficult, it's not who we are, it's just uncomfortable. Holding onto someone who can't do the job is hurtful to your organization. It's hurtful to the people who have to do the extra work to cover that person, and it's hurtful to the person because you're putting them in a position where they are never going to succeed."

Spirituality

When people are watching and emulating you, you have a responsibility to always strive to be your greatest self. There's an ancient Indian proverb, *"there is nothing noble in being superior to others. True nobility lies in being superior to your former self."* Even when you are at the top of your game if you want to continue to be great you have to constantly fine-tune your skills, not only in your field, but also spiritually. Leadership is a great responsibility and great leaders take it seriously by making their own evolution and growth a part of their daily lives.

I'm often asked how I transitioned from the legal field into executive coaching. The truth of the matter is it didn't happen right away. For about a year before I envisioned my work in the coaching field I knew I was unhappy in the music business. I wanted to make a change to a career where I was the client and my success was dependent upon my talents and skills instead of someone else's. I wanted to feel empowered and less dependent upon the success or loyalty of a third party. I love working with artists and creative people in general, but they are unpredictable and many of the executives at record companies are not pleasant. I wasn't having fun and the hustle started to feel too much like a hustle. I decided that I wanted my career, whatever that was going to be, to be dependent upon my growth as a spiritual being. I wanted the pressure of my own evolution to be the determining factor of my success. It's so funny because now when I am about to design a new workshop that requires me to embark upon unchartered territory, the Universe finds a way to give me the lesson I'm planning to teach ten times over prior to the actual workshop. Ready or not here it comes, bam! It's amazing because by the time I teach that workshop I have lived through the lesson, and I'm able to approach it and teach it from a place of pure intention. It's what I asked for and the Universe delivered. I love my work as a coach and I love the fact that the more I work on myself, the better I become at my job.

CHAPTER 6

Time, Balance, and Success

"The standard of success in life is not the things or the money - the standard of success is absolutely the amount of joy you feel."
Jerry & Ester Hicks, Ask and It Is Given

Success is something that you have to define for yourself, and your definition will change throughout different stages of your life. Today because I have a son in college, my definition of success has a lot to do with financial freedom and the ability to easefully provide for my son and cover my household expenses. It's also about experiencing peace, having a lover that I enjoy, and being in a position to give back and touch other people's lives. Each day that I'm able to be present and aware of my goodness and that of everyone else, is a good day.

Congresswoman Barbara Lee has devoted her life to service, and that's how she defines success. **"Success has nothing to do with money. Success is helping people along the way. If you use your life to enhance the life of others, and to lift people up, and to make sure that they have a secure life, then that is success."**

As you climb the ladder of success in your professional life, keep asking yourself one important question so that you stay connected to your higher Self and what really matters to you: "Am I enjoying my life?" No matter what your title is, how much money you have, or who you marry, if you are not happy then none of it matters.

Your Relationship To Time

The way you relate to, think about, and feel about time is directly related to how you relate to, think about, and feel about the quality of your life. Robert Sharma wrote, "As you live your days, so you live your life." If you feel overwhelmed by time, then you experience life as overwhelming. If you feel constantly hurried and lacking in time, then you experience life as slipping away and out of your hands. Most of us think of time in a linear fashion passing by with every minute, hour, and day. For many of you the soundtrack in your head related to time may sound something like this: "there's never enough time", "I need more time", "there aren't enough hours in the day", "If only I had more time", "where does time go?" These are the kinds of thoughts that perpetuate a competitive and anxious society. When we feel like there is only a limited amount of something, in this case a scarcity of time, we experience feelings of desperation and fear. It's nearly impossible to be innovative and creative from this space.

Then there's the issue of lateness. Some people are always late. It's true that different cultures have different views about time and how long is reasonable amount of time to keep a person waiting. However, in world of business late is late. There's a saying, "There's no such thing as on time; you are either early or you're late." Personally, I always prefer to be early rather than experience the feelings of anxiety that I come over me when I know someone is waiting for me. Whether it's business or personal, I don't like to keep people waiting and within reason, I don't like to be kept waiting. The general rule for personal affairs is that a fifteen-minute window is acceptable, but anything after that is considered late.

Lateness is a sign of many different things. On one hand, it's a sign of disrespect for others and the value of their time. This is an egocentric point of view and it implies that your time is more valuable than another's. On the other hand, some people are late because they believe their time, or even more sadly their presence, is of little or no importance. They have so little self-esteem that they believe it won't make a difference to the person or people waiting whether they show up on time or at all. If you are a person who tends to arrive late take a moment to reflect upon this important matter and ask yourself why. Why don't you allow yourself more time to prepare? Why don't you plan for possible contingencies, like traffic? Why is it ok to keep other people waiting? What is wrong with being early? Do you subconsciously believe that your on-time arrival doesn't matter? You may think your late tendencies are not a big deal, but they are. It becomes part of your reputation and that's not good, especially for business. There's a huge opportunity for growth and expansion in this one little trait alone.

Exercise

The next time someone keeps you waiting take a moment to document your thoughts. Monitor your level of anxiety, possible feelings of self-righteousness, or even anger. What did you think about the other person? How late were they, and what happened to your thoughts over time, 15 minutes, 20 minutes, 30 minutes. Did the person call or text you to let you know he or she was running late? What impact did the communication, or lack thereof, have on your thoughts and feelings? What did you do with your time while you were waiting? Did you immediately take out your smart phone and make yourself "busy"? If so, why? Did you feel like you had to be "productive" while you were waiting and anything else, as in just sitting and possibly even daydreaming, would have been "unproductive". Were you concerned about the other people in the room watching you wait? Why?

The next time you find yourself waiting, try not to pull out your cell phone. Try instead to use that time as an opportunity to practice mindfulness, to connect with your breath, and to be still. Try enjoying the down time. The more present we are, the more meaningful our entire lives become. In the words of J. Krishnamurti, "For the mind to be creative, there must be stillness." I now look forward to those times when I am able to arrive early for a meeting or dinner with friends so that I can sit still for a moment. It gives me time to collect my thoughts and assess my day. It gives me the space to mentally prepare for my meeting or look forward to my friend's arrival. It also gives me time to read or write, if I so desire. The one thing I try not to do is to surf my phone. I find that checking emails or looking through social media leave me feeling agitated and disconnected. Arrive early for your meetings and choose a new habit while you wait. Be creative and experience peace.

Like many working parents, it took the disappointment of Rich Kleiman's 6 year old daughter to make him change his cell phone habits. **"I believe**

I shut down on the weekends. My wife Jana may answer differently. It's not completely shutting down, but I try. Now that my six-year old daughter is old enough to tell me to put my phone away it makes a big difference. I never wanted that so now I'm shutting down. I'm good at setting boundaries. I don't have to answer an email for five hours. I can let the phone ring and unless it's urgent, I don't feel the need to call right back. For me that's the beginning of learning how to shut down."

Technology

We now live in a technological society that affords us instantaneous, non-stop access to stimulation and information from all around the world. While this presents a tremendous opportunity for growth and development, it also presents the disadvantages of over stimulation and confusion. Because of the availability of so much all the time, our ability to focus on one thing over a long period of time has suffered. The constant interruption of email, phone calls, posts, videos, photos, and tweets leads to mediocrity in everything. In fact, according to the Kleiner Perkins Caufield & Buyer's annual Internet trends report, people check their phones over one hundred fifty times per day. The truth is that all of this tuning in is causing us to miss out. We are missing a loss of connection. We're missing a loss of connection to ourselves and to each other. When you give your attention to one specific task at a time, not only will you find that you are more productive, you will also find that you experience more contentment.

There's also the problem associated with the kinds of information we are consuming on all of these screens we scan all day long. In 2012 the Media Violence Commission of the International Society for Research on Aggression, in its report on media violence said, "Over the past 50 years, a large number of studies conducted around the world have shown that watching violent television, watching violent films, or playing violent video games increases the likelihood for aggressive behavior." You have to be mindful of what you are watching. It does have an impact on your thoughts and your actions. It's ever so subtle, but it matters. If you want to experience peace, change the channel. Support musicians and artists who promote positive messages. Choose the other television program so that you sow the seeds of beauty, peace, and goodness in your life.

Exercise

No electronics for a full day. No email, surfing, text, posting, nada. You can answer the telephone but nothing else. The following morning document your experience.

Balance and Putting Yourself First

In increasingly stressful times, it's essential for you to develop a work plan that optimizes your health, manages stress, and balances work, family, and your personal life. You have to take care of yourself. It's the only way to develop the resiliency necessary for you to bounce back from setbacks and difficult times. If you're constantly overwhelmed and stressed out, your health will suffer and then you will be of no use to anyone. You have to learn the power of "no". People-pleasing is a form of martyrdom and it's not an admirable trait. I have a friend who is general counsel for a large federal agency and she works over seventy hours a week. Her famous lines are, "I have to go back to work" or "I have over 60 days worth of vacation time." That's not impressive, it's crazy. If she drops dead tomorrow, they will replace her without a second thought. Even the President of the United States takes vacations, and no one has more on his or her plate than the President.

Good leaders also don't get overwhelmed and stressed out because they make sure that they hire and train highly skilled workers and then, they allow them to do their jobs without micromanaging. They understand the importance of down time and relaxation and they insist upon it for themselves, as well as their employees. Happy, well-balanced people produce the best results.

You must exercise and take care of your body. It's your temple, and the only means through which you can experience your divine self. People who have hobbies they enjoy are happier people than those who don't. Even if you take a walk every day, that's great. If you want to stay vibrant and healthy you have to move around. Your exercises and sports don't have to be formal or competitive. It's so funny, many New Yorkers have found a way to turn even yoga into a competition. The few times I have taken a yoga class in New York City, the energy to me did not feel "yogic". It felt like the antithesis of yoga. New Yorkers can be so competitive that they have the ability to turn everything, even yoga, into a competition. Find what you love, the environment that suits you, and maintain a regular exercise practice.

Release your stress and ease your mind as you enhance your health and vibrancy.

It is equally as important for you to make the time to play and have fun. Everyone who knows me knows that I love to laugh. There's nothing like a good laugh. It feels good and it's good for you. Even the simplest little things can be fun and playful. Live your life subliminally. It's like smelling a flower. How do you smell a flower? It can't be hurried. It must be sublime. You gently close your eyes and take in the fragrance. While I was in India I realized that you actually watch and see the sun set, often surprisingly so. Most often you consciously plan to wake up early and watch the sun rise, but we usually don't bring the same level of awareness to the setting sun, and the two are uniquely different experiences. The more finely attuned you become to a sense of well-being, the more alert you will become to the things, the people, and the circumstances that magnify your contentment, as well as those that place it in jeopardy. You will begin to protect your happiness and your joy. It will become your compass.

Meditation

Meditation is that precious time and space that you give yourself to turn inward and rest. As you develop a regular meditation practice, ordinary life becomes a sacred existence. Meditation does what all of the therapy, pills, alcohol, workshops, and self-help books are not able to do. The purpose of meditation is inner happiness, inner peace. Instead of having negative thoughts, have the awareness, "I am pure, I am joy." Feel good about yourself. Fill yourself with great divinity. Meditation calms your mind. It's a respite from the constant thinking about tomorrow or what should have happened yesterday. Meditation whispers that all you have is today and that today, this moment, is all that matters. It will chase away your indifference, your apathy, the worries of your mind, and the disease of erratic thinking.

I began meditating over twenty-two years ago, and it has changed my life. It has shifted my sense of being. I now experience life with a different level of subtlety and awareness than I used to. I received shaktipat from Gurumayi Chidvilasananda, on August 12, 1995 at the Siddha Yoga Ashram in South Fallsburg, New York. There are many people in India and around the world who claim to be Gurus but when you receive the grace of a true Guru every fiber of your being tells you so. However, you don't have to receive the shaktipat or grace of a spiritual master to have a mediation practice. All you have to do is simply sit and acknowledge your own divine self. Even when your mind wanders, you are still meditating. It's during mediation that you make peace with your mind. You make peace with those aspects of yourself that you're not pleased with. You make peace with your negative thoughts. You make peace with your shame and other painful emotions that may surface so that you can move through them, heal, and experience wholeness. As you sit with the tenderness of your pure being you soften towards life. You become more loveable. You become more loving and as a result, you experience more joy.

    Chris Rock also has a daily meditation practice. *"I meditate"*, Chris told me. *"Meditation is just a pause. It's nice to pause every day. I try to meditate in the morning before all the noise. Even out here in Alpine the guys have leaf blowers or something. I try to get it in while it's nice and peaceful and serene. I can sit anywhere. It helps me with stress but if you're a writer stress is good for you in a lot of ways. You want to get it out through your work. Tension is good. I get it out through writing and performing."*

Develop a meditation practice for yourself. There are many courses and books on meditation that can help you as a guide. There are also thousands of people who teach meditation classes and offer courses and retreats all over the world. If there is someone whom you admire for their equanimity, ask them if they have a meditation practice. Chances are they do, and they can offer you some guidance to get started. However, please know that the simple act of sitting quietly with the intention of acknowledging your own divine self is the act of meditation. Create a sacred space in your home and sit comfortably. Sometimes it helps to watch your breath so that your mind stays calm. You may even repeat a mantra or something as simple as "I love myself" with the rhythm of your breath to help cool your anxiety. Please don't think of meditation as something that you have to learn to do, or that it's difficult. Even reading can be a form of meditation. When you study scriptures, what you're really doing is spending time in the company of great souls. A lot of people say they can't meditate simply because they can't sit still for a few minutes at a time. They believe they have to shut off their mind, but that is neither true nor possible. It's your mind's job to think. The problem with people who cannot sit still is that sitting still is so new to them, when they finally do their minds drive them crazy. They spend so much of their lives running from their mind, that the moment they stop running, they can't stand it. It's only by learning to sit still that you mind will finally calm down. Namaste.

CHAPTER 7

The Art of Giving

"To give charity in secret, to honor a guest, To be silent after doing good work, To speak openly of the good done by others, To be free from vanity in spite of wealth, And to speak well of others. These are the virtues generally possessed by good people."
Bhartrihari, the Niti Shataka

The fact that we need philanthropy is the problem with philanthropy. We have become a society that values money and things, more than human life. All of the grasping and possessing that we do is harmful. We live a self-centered existence and demonstrate a lack of responsibility for each other and the planet.

We all want the same things. We want the safety and the comfort of a home. We want easeful access to healthy food and clean water. We want our children to thrive and have access to the best education. We want love and connection. But our hearts have hardened. Instead of letting our suffering lead us to compassion and empathy for one another, we have hardened. We must transform our egocentric existence into something beautiful that benefits mankind so that we can uplift each other, stop all the wars, and know peace.

You Are Blessed

Philanthropy is not about feeling guilty about all the things that you have, or the ease in which you live your daily life. It is about realizing how blessed you are. It's about allowing that awareness to humble you and make you a more divinely compassionate human being. Jack Kornfield wrote, "It is the tender heart of a warrior that has the power to heal the world." It is that compassion which will guide you in your giving back. Many people dedicate their lives to service and helping others because it's their calling. True philanthropy has to be rooted in humanity. You must have a sincere desire to make a difference and to do good in the world. You must genuinely care about the well-being of other people. Your giving and your service have to be selfless. Your intention must be pure. In the name of humanity, find that pure place within yourself and make your philanthropy purposeful and intentional.

    Buddha found the practice of giving, known as "dana" or "dakshina" to be a good method for removing greed and attachment. In many of his discourses, he urged Buddhhists to practice dana wherever and whenever possible. He wrote,
"Just as a pot filled with water, if overturned by anyone, pours out all its water, and does not hold any back, even so, when you see those in need, whether low, middle or high, then give like the overturned pot, holding nothing back." Giving comes in many forms. As Congresswoman Barbara Lee put it, **"Some people do philanthropy because they get a tax credit. It's hard to criticize anyone's motives as long as they are doing what they should do. 'To Whom**

Much Is Given Much Is Expected.' For me, I just believe in the stuff. I want to change the world."

Chris Rock believes, "Your first job is to take care of your family. Most of us have extended family. My father has nine brothers and five sisters, each with at least five kids. I have over one hundred first cousins, on my father's side, ok. I help a lot of people, including aunts and uncles, so if I never wrote a check to any organization no one could say that I don't do any philanthropy. Sending your cousin to college is philanthropy. Paying the rent for someone you grew up with is philanthropy. All of that is giving to the community. It's nice to support a few organized charities, but don't frown upon people who are taking care of their family. A lot of people don't take care of their family and take that part for granted."

Aaron Walton believes, "We all have an obligation to leave more than we have taken. We do it in different ways. We can find ways that are fun and engaging. It doesn't always have to be about education. It depends upon your personal passion. For me it is not a 'nice to do, it's a 'need to do'. I want my legacy to be about, not selling more cars or more soap, but what I have been able to do with my power to help someone else, or to make the world a *better place. I tend to find myself attracted to other people who are like that."*

Richard Kleiman told me that he believes that giving back, no matter how you do it, is imperative. *"I wasn't given like Kevin Durant's been given but we all have our health and our experiences, and I like to give that. I spoke a few weeks ago to a senior class for Kevin's foundation. There were only about one hundred students in the room but I loved it. I didn't write anything down, I simply shared my experiences. Twenty or so kids emailed me afterwards. I give money when I can but more importantly, I like to touch people's lives. It gives you such a reality check. It makes you slow down and realize how fortunate you are."*

Personal Pilgrimage

I believe that in order to create genuine change, our hearts must change. In December 2007 my best friend, Yvette, and I went to India for a ten-day meditation retreat. We were with three other friends, one of whom, Harshada, also served as our tour guide. Harshada had previously lived in India for a couple of years as a devotee of Siddha Yoga Meditation. He spoke Hindi and knew the locations of some of the most ancient and revered villages and temples in India. Immediately upon arrival at the airport in Mumbai, it became clear to me that India was a country of people whose daily activities were second to their spiritual life. A country of over one billion people, most of whom possess very little, nevertheless, spend their days with an awareness of God's infinite grace. Catherine Ann Jones eloquently described India as "a mirror which intensifies whatever is reflected in one's self."

On the seventh day of our retreat, we were scheduled to travel for five hours in our minivan, South across the mountains from the countryside of Gangapur to a city called Allandi. As we quietly travelled along, I thought to myself how the mountains had a gentle texture to them, similar to the gentleness I was experiencing from the people. We had just finished a private, two-day silent retreat at an ayurvedic herb garden, so we were baked in stillness. The more you practice silence, even for a couple of hours a day, the more inner stillness becomes a part of your being, a part of who you are.

The purpose of our visit in Allandi was to take "a sweet pilgrimage", a madu yatra as it is called in Sanskrit, to the tomb of Jnaneswar Maraji. When you take a pilgrimage to a holy place it's to search for the knowledge of truth. It's said that to make real progress in one's spiritual practices, the grace of a great being is vital. Baba Muktananda once said, "There is a being inside you who knows everything." Jnaneswar was the brother and closest disciple of Nivrittinath, and a renowned Saint and Master throughout India. Just before our trip, Yvette and I finished a course with Harshada studying Jnaneswar's version of the Bhagavad Gita. It was part of what inspired the idea for our trip to India in the first place, so the timing of our visit to his tomb could not have been more auspicious. I felt a deep personal connection to Jnaneswar.

As we drove to his temple before sunrise the next morning, we passed hundreds of beautiful brown faces walking along the road; hundreds of men, women, children, and Sadhus of all ages, some wearing shoes, others without. It was early but the air was already warm. The women wore soft, flowing saris of crimson, orange, pink, yellow, violet, blue. Their silky black hair hung loosely or braided down their backs. As we continued to drive mile after mile toward the temple, I realized how far most of the people had come, and how far they still had to walk. No one seemed to mind. They walked along purposefully.

After driving for about thirty minutes, we arrived at the village where the temple was located.

In awe, I glanced at the line of people waiting to enter to receive Jnaneswar's blessings or "darshan", as it is called. The line stretched down the street as far as my eyes could see. There were thousands of people. As each person arrived at the temple, he or she silently took his or her place at the back of the line and waited dutifully to enter the tomb. No one showed the slightest hint of agitation. Peace permeated the atmosphere as each person joined the line in silent contemplation. It was astonishing. Everyone was so beautiful. I thought shamefully of the few times I had waited impatiently in line at the supermarket.

    Upon our arrival, we were escorted as "VIPs" past the line towards the rear. We were directed to the back entrance and seated among many beautiful holy men that are called "Sadhus" in India. Shortly thereafter we were escorted into the temple where we sat in the small room where the actual sacred lingum was located. The lingum is a physical stone located directly above Jnaneshwar's tomb so it is endowed with his grace. We were to participate, along with a couple of other great Sadhus, in the Abhishek. An Abisheck is a Hindu ritual of cleansing. It is a purifying ceremony usually accompanied by mantras, where you bathe the stone lingum located inside of the temple with water, milk, fruit, coconut, and any other juices available as an offering of reverence to the saint whose spirit resides there.

During darshan a seeker enters the sacred room where the lingum is located to receive Jnaneswar's blessing. We were seated in this actual room performing the Abhishek. As participants in the ceremony, we were directed to collect the sacred gifts of coconut, flowers, mangos, juices, and everything else presented from the villagers as they approached the room for Jnaneswar's blessings. We offered them on their behalf by positioning the items in the room or rubbing the liquid gifts on the lingum. As each man, woman, and child approached from the line, he or she was hastily pushed through by the attendants and given about ten seconds to make an offering. Even though many of the devotees had walked for days and stood in line for countless hours, the attendants dismissively rushed them through the temple. Unfortunately, they had no choice otherwise they would never get to the end of the line.

We sat there inside the small room and watched all of those people approach the temple with their hearts wide open. Slowly, as if awakening from a trance, I became conscious of how profound it all was. I was kind of in shock and overcome with the intensity of emotion that I had never experienced, and couldn't begin to comprehend. I started to feel waves of love. The tenderness was palpable. My heart began beating so fast I could hardly breathe. I began to gasp for air and tears poured from my eyes. I cried uncontrollably. I thought to myself, "What am I doing here? Why? Some of these people walked for days. They stood in line for countless hours. Ten seconds of grace, brushed off by the attendants, and here we were sitting for hours." At first it felt unendurably unfair. I felt that this was something I should not be allowed to see without the permission of these great souls as they entered the tomb. How could it be that we were sitting there witnessing thousands of people in their most loving divine state; Why us? Why me?

As the moments passed and the seekers continued to pour in, my conscious mind and my ego slowly began to fade and my heart took over. I now felt humbled beyond words. The exchange of love that I felt between us as the devotees continued to pass through the room was like nothing I had experienced before. Every offering they gave I wanted to give back to them ten-fold. The amount of love I felt was overwhelming. I cried and cried. I was so humbled and grateful. I took their offerings one by one and placed them or smeared them on the lingum. With each offering, I offered in return from the deepest part of my soul, my most sincere wish for joy and peace in their lives. I loved them and cared about them, and I wanted them to know it. I looked in their eyes and I knew that they would forever be a part of my life.

    This was soul connection. What I felt was radical empathy. In that moment of complete and utter surrender, I experienced a new, profound capacity for love and connection; a cleansing of consciousness, a purification, an awakening. Offering prayer and blessings for someone else changes your own heart. You become the love you offer. What I experienced and what I knew for sure in that moment on that day was that God was pleased with me. There was no other explanation. It was a sacred mystery.

    The subtle presence of divine beings never diminishes. When you give your adoration to a great being, what you are really celebrating is your own higher self. In the same way, when you genuinely care for another being, you are caring for God. That is true love, and your blessing in return is the grace of your own heart, the love of God, the merits of right action, and peace. As my friend Amol said the following day, "We must have accumulated great merit to have the blessings that we had yesterday."

Pay It Forward

If you change the course of just one person's life, you make a profound impact on the rest of society. As we "pay it forward" the world benefits one person at a time. It only takes one Archbishop Desmond Tutu, one Mahatma Gandhi, one Mother Teresa, one Gurumayi Chidvilasananda, one Martin Luther King, one Eleanor Roosevelt, one Abraham Lincoln, one Eckhart Tolle, one Maya Angelou, one Thurgood Marshall, one Winnie Mandela, one Barak Obama, one Tenzin Guyato His Holiness the Dalai Lalma, one Swami Muktananda to change the course of history.

The simple act of performing what is known as "a random act of kindness" has the power to elevate energy vibrations and lift our own and others spirits, as we go about our daily lives. Simply smiling, saying hello, or inquiring about someone's day with sincere interest are ways in which you can express kindness to another person. If we all cared about each other a little more, the world would be a sweeter place. Our hearts would soften and we would not be able to inflict suffering upon one another as we do today. When you have more compassion for yourself and your own suffering, you are naturally able to be more compassionate towards others. We must heal ourselves before we can heal the world.

There is a Cherokee Indian legend called *The Two Wolves*. It goes something like this:

A Native American grandfather is talking to his grandson about how he feels about a tragedy in their village.
"I feel as if I have two wolves fighting in my heart", he tells his grandson.
"One wolf is the vengeful, angry, violent one. The other wolf is the loving, compassionate one."
The grandson asks, "Grandfather, which wolf will win the fight in your heart?"
The grandfather places his hand on his heart and replies, "the one I feed."

What is the solution? You are the solution. It is about awareness and choice. So many of us live such insular lives where we seldom venture out of our comfort zones. We work with the same people and typically socialize with people who share our same values or economic status. Many of us do not even have more than two or three genuine friends of a different race. Humanity begins with choosing to see other people; to really look at their lives, their circumstances, and to imagine walking in their shoes.

Where ever you are there's always opportunity to make a difference. Philanthropy is about choosing in those moments to make a difference, to connect, and to do what you can no matter how small it may seem to you at the time. Some people are in the fortunate position to be able to do more than others. How much you are able to serve or to give is not the point. The intention of the doing is what makes the difference.

I believe in karma, lineage, and free choice. Where one starts out in life makes a tremendous difference. This is what you must remember if you begin to think that you are superior to, or better than any other human being. You must remember where you started, and that you are blessed. Some children are born in the slums of Mumbai, in a refugee camp outside of Syria, an orphanage in Ethiopia, or into a culture or religion that treats women as second-class citizens. Remember the circumstances of your birth, where it all began, and your blessings.

The following is a true story that I read while taking a writing course by Catherine Ann Jones:

A boy of five was asked by his parents if he would give blood to his three-year old sister, who might die without the right blood transfusion. The boy hesitated and then asked if he could decide the next morning.

"Of Course", his parents agreed.

The next morning the boy solemnly told them, "Yes, I will give my blood to my sister."

At the hospital, the little boy was on the gurney near his sister when the doctor came over to begin the transfusion process.

At that point, the little boy looked up at the doctor and asked, "How soon before I die?"

This story melts my heart every time I read it. These are the precious moments that I use as my love compass. The ease in which I am able to melt tells me that I am in my heart and that I am tender. Melting is how I know I am on my path. When was the last time you melted? As you go on your journey and become the tremendous success that is your destiny, do not forget to melt; stay soft, stay sweet, be kind, be good, and do good.

About the Author

Wendy Credle is a serial entrepreneur. She is an entertainment attorney, executive coach, television producer, and real estate agent. Her first forays into the corporate world were as an Executive Assistant, and A&R Director in the music industry. Six years later she went to law school and founded her boutique law firm, Credle & Associates, PLLC.

In 2012 Wendy's passion shifted and she founded Spanda Coaching, where she leads workshops and seminars for executives and corporations all over the world.

She was a cast member of the WEtv docu-series that featured 6 New York based, entertainment lawyers, entitled *Money.Power.Respect*. She is also the Executive Producer of a new docu-series for the Bravo Network about 6 married couples based in Charlotte, NC.

Wendy has spent the past 23 years of her life on a spiritual path traveling throughout India and spending time at the Siddha Yoga ashram in the Catskills.

Wendy holds a BS from the University of Michigan and a J.D. from Fordham University School of Law.

You can contact Wendy at spandacoaching@gmail.com

www.ingramcontent.com/pod-product-compliance
Lightning Source LLC
Chambersburg PA
CBHW031418290426
44110CB00011B/429